Oakley & Mason

Always be kind,
be optimistic,
Playful
   and
Protect the weak!

Debbie Spence

This book is presented to
Oakley & Mason Morales

by

Great-Grandma Judy and
Great-Grandpa Lou

on
December 23, 2024

All God's Creatures: 60 Days of Devotions for Animal-Loving Kids

Copyright © 2021 Little Lamb Books
Illustrations copyright © 2021 Katie Wekall

Edited by Lindsay Schlegel, *lindsayschlegel.com*
Designed by Katie Risor, *katierisor.com*

ISBN: 978-1-953456-00-7 (Hardcover)
ISBN: 978-1-953456-13-7 (Paperback)
ISBN: 978-1-953456-26-7 (eBook)
Library of Congress Control Number: 2021938639

Published by Little Lamb Books,
An imprint of Lamb Publishing, LLC
www.littlelambbooks.com
P.O. Box 211724, Bedford, TX 76095

All rights reserved. No portion of this book may be used or reproduced, stored in a retrieval system, or transmitted in any manner or by any means - electronic, mechanical, photocopy, recording, scanning, or other - except for brief quotations in critical reviews or articles, without the prior written permission of the publisher.

Unless otherwise noted, Scripture quotations are taken from the Holy Bible, New International Version, NIV. Copyright© 1973, 1978, 1984, 2011 by Biblica, Inc. Used by permission of Zondervan. All rights reserved worldwide. *www.zondervan.com* The "NIV" and "New International Version" are trademarks registered in the United States Patent and Trademark Office by Biblica, Inc.

The NIV and New International Version are trademarks registered in the United States Patent and Trademark Office by Biblica, Inc.

Little Lamb Books can connect authors to your live event.
Visit littlelambbooks.com for additional information and resources.

For information about special discounts or bulk orders, please contact Little Lamb Books at *orders@littlelambbooks.com*

First Edition
Printed in the United States of America

Little Lamb Books Presents

All God's Creatures

60 Days of Devotions for Animal-Loving Kids

Table of Contents

Introduction *Rachel Pellegrino* · · · · · · · · · · · · 8

Ant · 11

    Diligent *Tori Higa* · · · · · · · · · · · · · · · · · 12

    Strong for Its Size *Neena Gaynor* · · · · · · · · · 14

    Team Player *Shelly Roark* · · · · · · · · · · · · · 16

    Dependable *Jean Matthew Hall* · · · · · · · · · · 18

Bee · 21

    Foresight *Neena Gaynor* · · · · · · · · · · · · · · 22

    Sacrificial *Lindsay Schlegel* · · · · · · · · · · · · 24

    Responsible *Rachel Pellegrino* · · · · · · · · · · 26

Bunny · 29

    Gentle *Janelle Higdon* · · · · · · · · · · · · · · · 30

    Quiet *Neena Gaynor* · · · · · · · · · · · · · · · · 32

    Humble *Annette M. Clayton* · · · · · · · · · · · · 34

    Silly *Janet L. Christensen* · · · · · · · · · · · · · 36

Crocodile · 39

    Sneaky *Shelly Roark* · · · · · · · · · · · · · · · · 40

    Cranky *Rachel Pellegrino* · · · · · · · · · · · · · 42

    Mean *Suzanne Reeves* · · · · · · · · · · · · · · · 44

    Tough Skin *Patti Richards* · · · · · · · · · · · · 46

Dog 49
   Optimistic *Debbie Spence* 50
   Faithful *Amberly Kristen Clowe* 52
   Devoted *Jean Matthew Hall* 54
   Loving *Janet L. Christensen* 56

Dolphin 59
   Kind *Debbie Spence* 60
   Joyful *Shelly Roark* 62
   Willing to Learn *Amanda Flinn* 64
   Social *Janet L. Christensen* 66

Elephant 69
   Strong *Amberly Kristen Clowe* 70
   Reliable *Shelly Roark* 72
   Pack-Oriented *Amanda Flinn* 74
   Protects the Weak *Debbie Spence* 76

Flamingo 79
   Beautiful *Janelle Higdon* 80
   Self-Confident *Amanda Flinn* 82
   Spunky *Janet L. Christensen* . . . 84
   Graceful *Lindsay Schlegel* 86

Fox ... 89

- Quick *Jean Petersen* ... 90
- Curious *Jean Matthew Hall* ... 92
- Clever *Amanda Flinn* ... 94

Hippo ... 97

- Protective *Michelle Medlock Adams* ... 98
- Independent *Jean Petersen* ... 100
- Aggressive *Ashley L. Jones* ... 102
- Lives in Community *Annette M. Clayton* ... 104

Lion ... 107

- Leader *Amberly Kristen Clowe* ... 108
- Courageous *Neena Gaynor* ... 110
- Brave *Michelle Medlock Adams* ... 112
- Just *Patti Richards* ... 114

Octopus ... 117

- Intelligent *Suzanne Reeves* ... 118
- Perceptive *Burton W. Cole* ... 120
- Flexible *Annette M. Clayton* ... 122

Otter ... 125

- Friendly *Amberly Kristen Clowe* ... 126
- Energetic *Jean Matthew Hall* ... 128
- Playful *Debbie Spence* ... 130
- Creative *Tori Higa* ... 132

Panda	135
Distinctive *Ashley L. Jones*	136
Sensitive *Burton W. Cole*	138
Rare *Michelle Medlock Adams*	140
Climber *Patti Richards*	142
Sheep	145
Hopeful *Jean Petersen*	146
Obedient *Janelle Higdon*	148
Vulnerable *Ashley L. Jones*	150
Listener *Michelle Medlock Adams*	152
Zebra	155
Bold *Suzanne Reeves*	156
Stubborn *Jean Petersen*	158
Individual *Tori Higa*	160
Contributions	162
Works Cited	165
Traits Index	166
Scripture Verse Index	168

Introduction

God is so good. He created you and me to be full of interesting features and individual characteristics that mix together to make us unique. In the same way, God created animals, and not only gave them special traits that we can see with our eyes—like spots, spiky fur, or purple tongues—but He also gave them different characteristics that help them survive wherever they live and thrive no matter the challenges they face.

The devotions in *All God's Creatures: 60 Days of Devotions for Animal-Loving Kids* are written to help you to learn more about animals, to learn more about yourself, and to build your relationship with Jesus. Each page offers you a short, but important message, and then asks you to think about it, journal about it, and pray about it. Mixed in with these devotions are verses from the Bible and fun facts about the animals featured in each section.

You can read these devotions by yourself or with your parents, grandparents, or guardians. You can read them when you're eating breakfast, or you can read them before you close your eyes at bedtime. In whatever way you use *All God's Creatures: 60 Days of Devotions for Animal-Loving Kids*, I pray each entry encourages you to be like Christ.

Remember, you were created in the image of Jesus! And you were created for your own special purpose. There might be other kids who have brown hair or blue eyes or freckles, but there isn't anyone else just like you in the whole wide world.

I hope you know Jesus loves you just as you are. We should always strive to show kindness and compassion, to share joy and be patient, and to grow to be graceful and humble. These are all characteristics of Christ, and being more like Him is a good goal. When you give your heart to Him, you are a part of God's family forever.

I'm so glad you picked this devotional! Thank you!

Rachel Pellegrino
Founder & Publisher
Little Lamb Books

an **ANT** is

diligent

strong for its size,

a team player, and

dependable.

Be diligent in these matters; give yourself wholly to them, so that everyone may see your progress.

1 Timothy 4:15

An Ant Is
DILIGENT

Ants are diligent creatures by God's design. They show us how to keep busy, stay focused, and be persistent in completing tasks. They are constantly working hard toward accomplishing goals, like digging their tunnels. Ants stay laser focused. They don't get sidetracked, and they are not lazy.

Sometimes it can be difficult for us to be diligent like the ant. Hard work is not always fun. It can be hard for us to keep working in areas that are challenging for us. But if you want to learn something like how to ride a bike, you must be diligent. It takes practice before you can ride on your own. It's the same thing if you want to become an athlete, artist, teacher, astronaut, scientist, doctor, veterinarian, and more. What is the reward for diligence? Accomplishing something you couldn't have done without putting in the work!

The Bible is clear about the wisdom of being diligent in what you do, and it warns us about laziness. Of course, there are some times when you just need a break. That is more than okay. We all need to listen to ourselves and give ourselves needed rest. But our lives fall out of balance when that is the only thing we do. (This is

Ants live in colonies that are usually underground and are made up of several chambers connected by tunnels.

why your parents don't let you watch TV all day long.) Even God rested on the seventh day after creating the world and everything in it, to show us that we need to take time to rest as well.

If you want to get better at something that is important to you, you must be diligent like the tiny ant with big goals and a strong work ethic. Keep practicing. Keep trying. Keep moving forward. Take time to rest and ask God for help, encouragement, and strength as you go. He will give it to you, and He will be right there beside you on your journey.

Think

In what area of your life do you want to reach a certain goal? What steps can you take to arrive there?

Journal

Write about a time when you were diligent and met a goal that was important to you. Describe how it made you feel after you completed the work.

Pray

Dear God, thank You for giving me the ability to work hard and do my best. Please help me to be as diligent as the ants You created in all that I do. Amen.

I love you, Lord, my strength.

Psalm 18:1

An Ant Is

STRONG FOR IT'S SIZE

Have you ever noticed ants marching on the ground? If you aren't looking, you might miss them! Ants are tiny parts of God's creation. But just because they are small doesn't mean they aren't able to do big things.

When David was a small boy, the Israelites were camped on one hill. The Philistine army had pitched their tents on another. Within their camp was the fierce and mean giant, Goliath. The giant was so big and tall, he could barely fit through most of our doorways today! The Bible says that King Saul and all of the Israelite army were terrified. Who could defeat the giant?

David was just a shepherd boy. He didn't seem like much of a match for the huge man. However, when David went to face Goliath, David didn't feel so small. He was brave because he came in the name of the Lord, our strength.

One stone from David's sling struck Goliath's forehead and sent him tumbling to the ground. The boy, David, had won! Victory belonged to the Israelites! And it was all because one little shepherd knew that our strength comes from God.

God created ants capable of mighty things. They are able to pick up and move pieces

Ant colonies can consist of up to a million ants.

of food or sticks and leaves much larger and heavier than themselves. Since God made the tiny ant able to do so much, just think how much more capable He made you … when you unite yourself with Him.

Throughout our lives, there will be moments when we feel too small or too weak for the task at hand. We want to give up and say, "I can't!" Even adults experience this.

Thankfully, the giants we face today usually aren't battle-ready men that are almost ten feet tall. Most of the time, we need strength to deal with a big test, something hurtful a friend says, or losing a game. These things may feel bigger than we are, but we never have to face any difficult circumstance alone. Remember, our true strength comes from the Lord.

Think

Think about a time when you were afraid. How did you deal with it? How could trusting God help?

Journal

Write about or draw a picture of a time when God helped you in a difficult situation.

Pray

Dear Lord, You are mighty and able to defeat any giant. Thank You for making me strong in You. Amen.

Just as a body, though one, has many parts, but all its many parts form one body, so it is with Christ.

1 Corinthians 12:12

An Ant Is
A TEAM PLAYER

Ants are everywhere! I'm sure you've seen ants in your yard, on the playground, maybe even in your house. Scientists say ants have colonized almost every land mass on earth. Some ant colonies even work together to form super colonies that consist of millions and cover vast amounts of land. Ants get things done!

What is the key to their success? Teamwork.

Each ant has a specific job and works together with other ants for the success of the colony. For example, some ants are tasked with the job of finding food for the colony, while others clean the nest and remove rubbish. There are ants who take care of recently hatched eggs and those who keep the nest safe from predators. Still others collect materials to improve the nest or maintain the tunnels. The queen ant has a specific job of laying eggs and increasing the population.

No job is too small. Ants depend on each other and each one works diligently for the good of the team. When they work together, ants are a mighty force of nature. They combine efforts to forage for food and build networks of tunnels.

You and I can also accomplish incredible (even impossible!) things when we work

Ants move more soil than any other organism, including earthworms.

together as a team. Scripture says that God has given each of us a specific gift or task as part of *His* team. Maybe your job is to encourage others with kind words or be a helper to someone who is struggling. Whether you sing and dance, draw or write, organize things or love to build, God can use your skills, along with those of others, to make big things happen.

Teamwork is not about just your specific gifts and abilities. It's also about attitude. Being a good team player means supporting your team members. It means working hard and doing your best, no matter what your job.

You are a critical part of God's plan. By being a good team player, you'll see His hand at work everywhere and be surprised at what you can accomplish!

Think

Recall some teams that you have been on (consider sports, group projects, your family) and what your roles have been.

Journal

Make a list of the gifts, talents, and special characteristics God has given you.

Pray

Dear God, thank You for the gifts and talents You have given me. I know that as I grow, I will discover even more. Guide me to use them for Your work. Amen.

*Go to the ant, you sluggard; consider its ways and be wise!
It has no commander, no overseer or ruler, yet it stores its
provisions in summer and gathers its food at harvest.*

Proverbs 6:6-8

An Ant Is
DEPENDABLE

The book of Proverbs tells us to watch the ants as they gather food and prepare for winter. They work. All. The. Time. Ants don't wait for someone to build their homes for them. They dig one tiny bit of dirt at a time to make their complex tunnels underground.

If you lie in the grass and watch ants, it may seem they are going nowhere. But if you follow their trails, you'll see they are busy harvesting seeds and grains to store away in their homes. A long string of ants marches off to find food. Then that same string marches back to their anthill with each one carrying as much as it can. They work all through the nice weather so they will have enough food saved up when snow or ice covers the ground.

Ants don't wait around to see if someone else will do the work. They all help. If every ant wants to eat and stay warm and dry, then every ant needs to work. They don't even wait to be told what to do. They see a job that needs doing, and they do it.

Can your parents depend on you to *always* make your bed without their nagging? Can your teacher depend on you to *always* complete and turn in your homework? Can your friends depend on you to keep your word and *always* have their backs?

There are more than 22,000 species of ants living on the Earth today.

Being dependable shows others that we care for them. It shows that we put them before ourselves—like Jesus did when He left the glories of heaven and came to earth as a helpless baby. Jesus put our needs before His own, not to be famous, but because He wanted us to have salvation.

We should be dependable because God is dependable. Pay attention to the ants. They can always depend on each other. Can other people depend on you?

Think

What are some things you can do to show others you are dependable and faithful to them?

Journal

Who in your life shows you that you can depend on them? How do they show you that?

Pray

Dear Lord, thank You for being my faithful Savior, who died on the cross for my sins. Help me to be someone You and other people can depend on. Amen.

foresight,

is sacrificial, and

is responsible.

"For I know the plans I have for you," declares the Lord, "plans to prosper you and not to harm you, plans to give you hope and a future."

Jeremiah 29:11

A Bee Has FORESIGHT

Honey bees are busy, buzzy little bugs. They spend their entire lives working to prepare for the winter. The survival of the whole bee family depends on it!

No one reminds the bees that they need to gather and store food while it's sunny. God just gave them this special instinct—or natural knack—for knowing what they need to do. The bees know that after summer, the coming winter could be difficult for them, so they prepare for it. He's given us this same gift of knowing what might happen in the future. We call it foresight.

We know that dark, cloudy days could mean rain is coming. So what do we do? We act with the knowledge that there *might* be rain, and we pack an umbrella. We also use foresight when we study for school or learn to ride a bicycle. We know that, someday, our teacher will probably give us a test or we will want to ride bikes with friends.

It's hard to think about what might happen and how we can plan for tomorrow, next weekend, or even next Christmas. The only one who really knows the future is God. Thankfully, He sent His Son, Jesus, to tell us how we can prepare for forever. We can practice

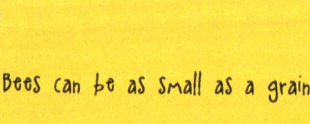

Bees can be as small as a grain of rice.

foresight now by focusing on our eternal life in heaven. That's right! We can have foresight to follow Jesus' example today for a happy forever. It's the one thing we can be sure of—that we can put all our trust in Jesus.

Like the bees in winter, we will all experience difficult times. We can plan and prepare, but the best way to practice foresight isn't by storing skills, a bunch of knowledge, or even jars of honey. It's by spending time with Jesus and trusting Him. The moments we spend with Him by reading our Bibles, praying, and thanking God for the beautiful gift of creation will give us exactly what we need for every season … and forever.

Think

Consider God's plan for you, to give you hope and a bright future. How can you practice foresight and act with care for tomorrow, next month, or even next year?

Journal

Write about or draw how you already use foresight at home, at school, or in your activities.

Pray

Dear God, thank You for having a wonderful plan for me. Help me to have the foresight to act in ways that are pleasing to You. Amen.

Greater love has no one than this:
to lay down one's life for one's friends.

John 15:13

A Bee Is
SACRIFICIAL

A worker honeybee is as dedicated to its work as it can get. The bee's job has three parts: gathering nectar, pollinating flowers, and defending the hive. It takes the last part of the three so seriously that if something threatens its hive, the bee will give its life for it.

Only worker honeybees are able to sting, and when they do, they usually die within ten minutes. The stinger that gets lodged in your skin pulls part of the bee's body apart, so that it can't survive. Why does the bee do it? To protect the other bees and the hard work they've put into creating and maintaining their hive.

It's this kind of all-out dedication that we are called to give to others, following Jesus' example. Jesus made a choice to give Himself up to save us from our sins. It wasn't easy, and in fact, the night before He died, He asked God the Father if He really had to do it. In the next breath, He gave Himself over to the Father's will. He surrendered His whole life for love of all of us. For me. For you.

It's unlikely that we will be called to physically die for another person in our lives. But we can choose to die to ourselves in little ways in order to serve others. You might choose to read a story

Honey bees dance to communicate information about finding food and new homes.

to a younger sibling, instead of starting the game you want to play. You could choose to put your laundry away without being asked, instead of running outside to meet a friend. You could choose the smaller cookie on the tray, leaving the bigger one for another family member to enjoy.

Little sacrifices like these aren't always seen by others, but God knows—and rejoices—when you put others before yourself. When we make choices like these into habits, we become more and more like Christ Himself. And when we grow in love like His, we invite others to do the same.

Think

What are some ways you can sacrifice yourself for someone else today?

Journal

When have you experienced someone sacrificing him or herself for your sake? How did it make you feel?

Pray

Dear Lord, thank You for making the ultimate sacrifice out of love for me. Help me to honor Your gift by making small sacrifices for people in my life. Amen.

Whoever can be trusted with very little can also be trusted with much, and whoever is dishonest with very little will also be dishonest with much.

Luke 16:10

A Bee Is
RESPONSIBLE

A hive of bees is like a family. Each member has a responsibility or a chore that it must complete. There are pollen collectors and hive protectors, family nurturers and home builders. Not one buzzy bee is too small or left out. They work together every day to accomplish their tasks, which brings harmony to their home.

But if one bee decided to stop being responsible and didn't collect pollen or chose not to protect the hive from predators, every single member of the hive—from the queen bee to the honey bees—would suffer. Why? Because each bee's job is important. They all have to do their individual parts to make their home the best place to live.

In your home, you are probably given your own responsibilities, like washing the dishes, taking out the trash, or feeding your dog or cat. These chores might not seem like a big deal to you. Sometimes you might not want to do your chores, because playing video games or playing outside with friends would be more fun. But if you were irresponsible and did not do your chores, you would not have clean dishes to eat on. The trash would pile up and be stinky. The animals would be hungry and sad.

Scientists have learned that honey bees know the world is round!

Jesus told His disciples that those who are responsible in the small things can be trusted with bigger things. When you are a part of a family, your responsibilities, even the smaller ones, teach you how to be a person who can help with bigger things. Every action you do with love helps to grow God's kingdom—in your home, your community, and the whole world.

Showing that you can be responsible is a way of loving your family, as if your home were a beehive!

Think

What are you responsible for in your home? How does doing your chores make a positive impact on those around you?

Journal

Write about a job that you don't like doing, but that you feel good about doing once it's completed.

Pray

Dear Lord, thank You for giving me talents and skills that can bless others. Please help me bring You glory by being responsible in my family, my school, and my community. Amen.

a **BUNNY** is

**gentle,
quiet,
humble, and
silly.**

*Be completely humble and gentle;
be patient, bearing with one another in love.*
Ephesians 4:2

A Bunny Is
GENTLE

Bunnies hop. Their feet flip flop. Noses wiggle, fluffy tails waggle. They zig zag through the grass and slip into the bushes quietly. Instead of being rough and tough, they are soft and gentle creatures. The sweet spirit of a bunny is a good example of how we, as followers of Jesus, should act.

When you're upset with someone, should you kick and scream? Nope. Should you hit your friends on the playground? Or say unkind things? Nope.

When bunnies are upset, they often twitch their tail or ears, but they don't lash out. They stay gentle with those around them.

Next time you're upset, take a deep breath and be gentle with your words and with your body. If it helps, try wiggling your ears like a bunny to help you calm down. Being gentle helps us to bear with one another in love. In other words, it helps us to show Jesus's love to our friends, family, and neighbors.

Gentleness is also a sign that we have the Holy Spirit in us. It is what the Bible calls a fruit of the Spirit. As you get to know Jesus better, trust in Him, and ask for His Spirit to be with you and help you.

Some cottontail bunnies have white shapes on their foreheads called stars or blazes.

Jesus is another great example of gentleness. He was the kindest, most tender person to ever live on the Earth. He was always patient with those around Him, and He treated them with care. He showed love and gentleness to people that others had a hard time loving.

The gentleness of the bunny helps us remember how to be soft and loving toward our friends and family, just like Jesus was. If you're feeling upset and want to yell or act out in a rough way, pray and ask God for help. Think about a sweet little bunny hopping through the flowers. Take a deep breath. Over time, God will grow your soft, bunny-like heart of gentleness.

Think

How can I show gentleness to my family and friends?

Journal

Give an example of a time when someone was gentle to you. How did it make you feel?

Pray

Dear Lord, help me to be gentle with my friends and family, even when I'm feeling frustrated or upset. Make my words and my actions gentle like a bunny's. Amen.

Rather, it should be that of your inner self, the unfading beauty of a gentle and quiet spirit, which is of great worth in God's sight.

1 Peter 3:4

A Bunny Is
QUIET

God made the rabbit to be quiet for a reason. The natural habitat for bunnies can be very dangerous. Being quiet allows them to listen, their long ears tuned in to the most important sounds around them.

Thankfully, people don't have to worry about all the things little bunnies do, but it's still important to have moments of quiet when our ears are open to listen.

It can be hard to be still and quiet when a baby is napping, when you are sick, or while visiting a library. But there is usually an important reason for why we are asked to be quiet. Babies who wake up too early are fussy. They don't get the rest they need in order to grow. When we are sick, our bodies need to rest and be still so they can be healthy again. Libraries are quiet so people can focus on reading and learning.

Being quiet also means we are ready to listen. God wants us to honor our parents. One way to do that is by listening to their instructions. We should also listen to our teachers, our coaches, and the many helpful adults who want to keep us safe.

Why else can it be important to be quiet and listen? Good friends listen. We've all had days when we just wanted to talk to someone.

Rabbits can see behind themselves without turning their heads.

It feels good to tell about our hard days or the great things that have happened to us. It would be frustrating if no one listened! That's why it's important for us to take turns and be the listener. Listen and learn how to be a better friend, a kinder brother or sister, or a more thoughtful teammate.

Sometimes God uses the Bible, prayer, or praise music to speak to us. As we see in the variety of amazing animals He made, God isn't limited in the ways He can communicate with our hearts. But we must be quiet. We must be still and listen. By being quiet and turning our ears to God, we will become better friends with Jesus and hear His every whisper.

Think

Who in your life is a good listener? What do they do that makes you know they are listening?

Journal

Writing or drawing is one way to be still. On your page, thank God for His blessings or ask for His help. He always hears our prayers … even when they're on paper.

Pray

Dear Lord, help my soul to be quiet, so that I may hear Your voice. Thank You for always listening to my prayers. Amen.

Who is wise and understanding among you? Let them show it by their good life, by deeds done in the humility that comes from wisdom.

James 3:13

A Bunny Is
HUMBLE

Soft, cuddly, and often shy, bunnies are humble animals. Being humble sometimes gets a bad reputation. Some people think it means being weak or passive. But this couldn't be further from the truth: humble people are often very confident! They know their worth from the tops of their heads down to the tips of their toes.

On the other hand, those who brag or boast about their talents, wealth, or knowledge often lack self-confidence. Deep down, they are seeking approval and validation from others because they don't believe in themselves.

God tells us to value others above ourselves. With confidence and humility, you can learn to put the needs of others before your own. This doesn't mean you shouldn't speak up for yourself; rather, if you are in a position of power, you should show generosity towards those who look up to you.

You may think that as a child, you are never in a **position of power**, but there are times when your **peers are looking** up to you! Pretend you're on the soccer team and you scored the winning goal. Instead of boasting about being the best player on the team, a true leader will show humility when being

Cottontail rabbits are more active at dawn and dusk.

congratulated by simply saying, "thank you" and "it was a team effort." Sharing the credit doesn't mean you value yourself less. Instead, it means sharing the excitement with others and spreading joy.

Along with being humble, bunnies are also very happy. When they get excited, bunnies do a move called the "binky." They jump into the air and twist and turn like a person might leap for joy and yell, "Yippie!" Being humble like a bunny can make you a happier person too.

Sometimes we forget to be humble bunnies when we get excited about our accomplishments. It's okay to have pride in something you have worked hard to achieve, but it is important to be mindful of others' feelings.

Next time you see a friend feeling left out when you did better than they did on a test or on the playing field, try comforting them, letting them know you think they are great and are proud of their hard work.

Think

What do you know about your worth as a child of God? How can you share your talents with others to make them feel special too?

Journal

Think about a time you did something really well and others felt upset that they didn't do the same. How did you react to their sadness?

Pray

Dear Lord, help to me practice humility by being self-confident, but not boastful. Guide me to be grateful for what I have and mindful of others' feelings. Amen.

Listen, my son, to your father's instruction and do not forsake your mother's teaching.

Proverbs 1:8

A Bunny Is
SILLY

Bunnies can be so silly! The other day I watched one as it was eating. It wasn't nibbling on grass. It was hopping from one fluff-topped dandelion to the next. It bit the dandelion off near the ground, just like you or I would do if we were going to pick it. Then it nibbled, nibbled, nibbled up from the bottom. It looked like the bunny was slurping up a string of spaghetti! It nibbled the stem all the way to the fluffy seeded top until *poof*, all the seeds went flying to the ground like fireworks in the sky. Then the bunny hopped on to the next dandelion treat and did the same thing. How silly!

It is fun to be silly sometimes. You might spin around in circles until you are dizzy or sing a song in a really silly voice. Being silly can make other people smile and bring them joy.

But being silly can also be a bad thing, especially if we get so caught up in being silly that we forget to listen to the wise instruction of the adults God gave us to take care of us. When one of these adults says it is time to stop being silly, we need to listen to their instruction. It may keep us from getting hurt.

What if one of those times we were spinning in circles and we lost our balance

Wild rabbits try to escape predators by running in a zig-zag pattern.

and fell, hitting our heads? That wouldn't be fun at all. It is a good thing that God gave us adults to take care of us and to help us know when it is no longer a good idea to be silly.

Thank you, God, for this special gift.

Think

Who are the adults God gave you to take care of you and to help you make good decisions? How can you show them that you respect their instruction?

Journal

Write about a time when you or someone you know was silly. Did it bring you joy? Or did someone end up getting hurt?

Pray

Dear God, thank You for helping me know when it is safe to be silly and for giving me people to help me know when acting silly is not safe for me. Amen.

a **CROCODILE** is

sneaky,

cranky,

mean, and

has tough skin.

Jesus turned and said to Peter, "Get behind me, Satan! You are a stumbling block to me; you do not have in mind the concerns of God, but merely human concerns."

Matthew 16:23

A Crocodile Is

SNEAKY

Crocodiles are sneaky. Have you ever had trouble spotting one at the zoo, no matter how hard you looked? Just because you didn't notice a crocodile right away doesn't mean it wasn't there. Crocodiles are experts at deceit and concealing themselves.

Crocodiles spend a lot of time with most of their bodies submerged underwater. Often, only their eyes and part of their snouts stick out, which makes them hard to see. Crocodiles have a special feature in their eyes that allows them to focus in a horizontal line even with the horizon, unlike other animals that focus better on a single point. This unique characteristic allows them to see everything in front of them without moving their heads. That way, they can stay perfectly still while waiting for prey. When the sun goes down, night vision gives them the ability to hunt under cover of darkness.

These toothy critters can also stay completely hidden underwater. They've been known to submerge completely for up to two hours without coming up for a breath! To accomplish this amazing feat, crocodiles slow their heart rate to just two beats per minute and save on the use of oxygen in different parts of their bodies. From

Crocodiles have been living on Earth since the time of the dinosaurs.

underneath the water, the stealthy hunters ambush unsuspecting animals who have come to the water's edge to drink or bathe. Other times the crocodile is hiding in plain sight, camouflaged as a log or other element of its environment.

The Bible says you and I have an enemy that is pretty sneaky, too. In the Gospels, we learn that Satan wants to draw us away from God by having us focus our minds and hearts not on the Lord who loves us, but on the passing things of the world. Fortunately, there is a way for us to recognize Satan and his works, and that is by knowing God's Word.

Scripture is like a spotlight on a spiritual crocodile who is waiting to sneak up on us. When we learn the stories of the Bible, we develop a powerful weapon against being sneaked up on as we grow up.

Think

How might Satan try to sneak up on you and cause you to stumble in your faith? What can you do to stop it?

Journal

Have you ever been caught off guard by someone who is mean to you? What made it so surprising?

Pray

Dear God, thank You for your love and protection. Please help me to hold Your Word in my heart so I won't be caught off guard by Satan's ways. Amen.

Rejoice in the Lord always. I will say it again: Rejoice!

Philippians 4:4

A Crocodile Is
CRANKY

Crocodiles are really big reptiles that have a large v-shaped jaw full of sharp teeth. Because of the way their jaws and mouths line up, when you see crocodiles up close, they sometimes look like they are frowning. Their appearance makes them look like they are cranky all the time!

Being cranky as a human can mean that you're acting out, frowning, or being mean to those around you. Maybe you've said hurtful words to others or you've taken a toy from a friend, or maybe you just feel frustrated with your day and don't want to be around others.

There are many reasons to feel cranky, but the Bible tells us that we should, "Rejoice in the Lord." No matter how our day is going, the hard stuff is temporary.

Whatever situation you are facing may not be full of joy, but *you* can be full of joy. You can sing worship songs, write in your journal, send a card or letter to a friend, bake cookies, or find an activity that will lift your spirits and help you remember that "the joy of the Lord is your strength."

Crocodiles can grow to over 23 feet in length and weigh over 2,200 pounds.

It's okay to have days when you feel down and don't feel like smiling, but remember that you can give those days to the Lord and trust Him with your heart. He rejoices in who He made you to be, and you can lean on Him for your joy.

Think

Think of someone you can always count on to cheer you up. What would he or she tell you to do to feel joyful on a cranky day?

Journal

Write about a time when you helped a family member or friend feel better after a tough day or a challenging situation.

Pray

Dear Lord, thank You for making me unique and for giving me Your joy even on the hard days. Lift my spirit and help me to be thankful for the many blessings in my life today. Amen.

Get rid of all bitterness, rage and anger, brawling and slander, along with every form of malice.

Ephesians 4:31

A Crocodile Is

MEAN

With its rows of razor-sharp teeth, its leathery skin, and its appetite for eating other animals, the crocodile isn't known for being warm and fuzzy. In fact, crocodiles can be mean!

Sometimes we are mean, too. We say hurtful things to our friends, making fun of them or putting them down. We snap our big teeth and take someone's toy or refuse to share ours. And just like other animals may run when they see the crocodile coming, our friends may run from us also. No one wants to be around someone who is mean.

But we can choose not to be mean. Instead of making fun of a friend, we can choose to say something nice. Instead of giving someone a shove on the playground, we can choose to help them carry their bag. If we see someone needs a place to sit on the bus, we can give them a smile, scoot over, and share our seat. Jesus told us to be kind to others. He told us to look for ways to encourage our friends.

Sometimes being mean is easier than being kind. But that doesn't mean it's okay. If you've been mean to someone, it's time to tell God you're sorry and ask Him to forgive you. And the good news is He will! You should apologize to

When a crocodile is about to hatch, it makes a chirping sound to let its mother know.

the person you were mean to as well. That can be really hard, but God will help if you ask Him to.

Every day we're faced with the choice to be kind or to be mean. When you want to snap your great big teeth, take a deep breath and maybe do a dive into the mud until you cool off. Choose to be kind, not mean. That might make even the crocodile smile.

Think

When was someone mean to you? How did it make you feel? What do you wish they would have done instead?

Journal

Think of a situation when you might feel like being mean. How can you choose to be kind instead?

Pray

Dear God, please forgive me for the times I have been mean to others, and help me to forgive others when they've been mean to me. Amen.

Be strong and courageous. Do not be afraid or terrified because of them, for the Lord your God goes with you; he will never leave you nor forsake you.

Deuteronomy 31:6

A Crocodile Has
TOUGH SKIN

When God gave crocodiles their skin, He knew that these scary, water-loving reptiles would need something extra special to help them survive in tropical places like Africa, South America, and southern Florida. Even though crocodiles are fierce and will eat just about anything with fins or four legs, they have their own set of predators to worry about. Lions, jaguars, tigers, and leopards are all capable of taking down a crocodile, and that's where the thick skin comes into play.

Crocodile skin looks very different from the skin of other animals, because the crocodile has horny scales in rows inside bony plates on its back and tail. There's a ridge on each horny scale. There are also small, knobby scales on its sides. Basically, a crocodile has a nice suit of armor that goes everywhere it goes!

The only skin on a crocodile that isn't covered in bony scales is the belly. That's why you'll never see a crocodile lying on its back in the sun. The crocodile's amazing thick skin makes it hard for other animals to attack and eat it.

You may have heard the expression, "She has a thick skin!" That doesn't mean a human's skin is

Crocodiles prefer to live near each other, rather than alone.

thicker than someone else's or that her body is covered in bony scales like the crocodile's. What it does mean is that person is not easily offended and she has courage even when faced with challenges or disappointments. Often this comes from trusting in God's love.

Like the crocodile, you are protected from all the hard things that might come your way, because you know your Heavenly Father watches over you and cares for you. He wraps you in His strong arms and protects you always, not just when you fall off your bike or get your feelings hurt by a friend. Growing this kind of "skin" takes trusting Him over and over and recognizing that no matter how hard things get, He is always there.

Maybe knowing it has all those bony scales protecting it is why the crocodile seems to be smiling. Take a moment right now to think about how much you are loved and protected by God. I'm sure it will make you smile too!

Think

What other animals did God give just-right traits to help them survive in their habitats?

Journal

When have you recognized God's protection during a tough time? What gift did God give you to help you through it?

Pray

Dear God, thank You for having me in the palm of Your hand, no matter what challenges or problems come my way. Help me to remember You are always near. Amen.

a **DOG** is

**optimistic,
faithful,
devoted, and
loving.**

May the God of hope fill you with all joy and peace as you trust in him, so that you may overflow with hope by the power of the Holy Spirit.

Romans 15:13

A Dog Is
OPTIMISTIC

When dogs play ball, they excitedly and eagerly wait for you to throw. Sometimes they jump around, doing their own kind of happy dance, certain that at any moment you are going to throw the ball. These optimistic pets are hopeful and confident that soon they will be racing across the yard to catch their favorite toys.

The happy, tail-wagging, ball-catching dog is a great example of an optimist. Optimists expect good things to happen. They usually have a positive attitude. The opposite of optimistic is pessimistic. Pessimists tend to see the worst side of things or believe the worst will happen.

Most dogs are loved by their owners and so they have been trained to trust that they will be treated well. Dogs that live in loving homes know that their owners will take care of them and love them, and in return they reward their human friends with wagging tails and sloppy kisses.

Just like the dogs who have loving, kind owners, we have a loving, kind God. We can trust our God because He always does what is best for us and always loves us. We can depend on Him. The Bible is full of promises about how He will be good to us. Because we

Dogs can hear sounds four times farther away than humans.

have a God that is always for us and never against us, we too can be optimistic about life. We can also be strong and courageous because He promised us that He will be with us wherever we go.

Pessimists can be fearful people. They always think something bad is going to happen. But God told us to not be terrified or discouraged. Sometimes things do not turn out as we want them to, and sometimes bad things happen. Life will not be perfect, but God is perfect. The Holy Spirit lives inside us, helping us to have joy and peace and to trust God even in the midst of difficult times.

Optimists are not hopeful and positive because things always look good; they are hopeful and positive because they trust God. The Bible shows us over and over that we can and should trust Him. Pray and ask for help to be optimistic when you are feeling low. Then just like the optimistic dog, you can do your own happy dance.

Think

Self-talk is the collection of thoughts you think about yourself. Is your self-talk positive or negative? How can you improve your self-talk?

Journal

Are you more optimistic or pessimistic? Write down why and list five ways you can trust God.

Pray

Dear Lord, thank You for being with me wherever I go. Please help me to trust You and to have joy, peace, and hope, and to believe the best can happen. Amen.

For we live by faith, not by sight.

2 Corinthians 5:7

A Dog Is
FAITHFUL

The Lord gave the world so many precious animals, and they are particularly sweet as babies! I love to be at the park in spring, when I might see ducklings following a mother duck, turtle hatchlings cracking through their eggshells, and tadpoles sprouting legs. Baby animals, like kittens with their little paws and bunnies with their twitching noses, are so cute.

But none of those animals is my favorite. My very favorite baby animal in the whole world is a puppy. I love their little snouts. I love their fluffy fur. And I really love their gentle barks. I could get puppy kisses all day! It's hard to believe that these teeny-tiny animals grow up into adult animals, but they do.

God made such neat animals when He made dogs. They are wonderful companions. They are so happy to spend time with their owners, playing games like fetch and roll over. It's no surprise dogs are known as "man's best friend." Some dogs will sit at the door all day, just waiting for their owners to return from places like work and school.

That dog who is waiting for its owner doesn't have to see him to know he will be back. The dog trusts his

Dogs use their wet noses to determine the direction of the air current that contains the smell they are following.

friend. There's a five-letter word that means something a lot like that: faith.

As Christians, we may not be able to see Jesus like we see Mom and Dad, but we know He really lived a perfect life. We know He died on the cross for us. And we know He will come back one day!

How amazing that God gave us dogs, and how lovely it is to have faith in Jesus!

Think

Do you need to see Jesus to believe in Him?

Journal

Write a sentence or two about what faith means to you.

Pray

Dear God, I pray that I learn more and more about Jesus and that my faith in Him grows stronger and stronger. Amen.

Commit to the Lord whatever you do, and he will establish your plans.

Proverbs 16:3

A Dog Is
DEVOTED

Guide dogs for visually impaired people are totally devoted to helping and protecting their owners. They stop at busy streets. They go around rocks and holes. They step between their owners and strangers. They pull their owners away from danger.

Similarly, police dogs are one hundred percent devoted to obeying their handlers' commands and to protecting their handlers from dangerous people or situations—even from knives and bullets.

If you have a dog of your own, I'll bet it follows you around wherever you go. If you're playing outside, your dog chases the ball with you. If you're watching a movie, your dog is probably curled up beside you or maybe in your lap. Maybe your dog sleeps with you at night. Even if you fuss at it, or punish it, your dog comes right back to you with that sad face that says, "I'm sorry. Do you still love me?"

That's because dogs are devoted to their owners. Your dog is devoted to you, wanting your touch, your attention, your words of praise, your love, no matter what.

The Bible gives us many examples of people who were devoted. Moses was

Nearly half of all homes in the United States have a dog.

devoted to leading the Israelites. Ezra was devoted to studying God's Word. King Solomon was devoted to building a beautiful temple for God. Nehemiah was devoted to rebuilding the Jerusalem wall. Paul was devoted to spreading the gospel of salvation.

To what, or to whom, are you devoted? Are you devoted to Jesus? Do you want to be near Him? To read His Word and hear His voice? To spend time with Him? If you're not sure how to do this, talk to your parents, your pastor, or your Sunday School teacher about how you can become more devoted to Jesus.

Just like you enjoy having your dog near you and spending time with you, God enjoys your spending time with Him. Do you know why? Because He's devoted to you, too.

Think

> What are some synonyms for, or other words that mean the same thing as, "devoted"?

Journal

> What do you devote your time and energy to? Athletics? Church? Bible study? Your family? Good grades? Why are you devoted to these things?

Pray

Dear Lord, change my heart and make me devoted to You, to reading Your Word, and to talking with You in prayer each day. Amen.

Keep on loving one another as brothers and sisters.

Hebrews 13:1

A Dog Is
LOVING

I have a dog that loves me no matter what. He loves me when I am happy. He loves me when I am sad. Whenever I sit down, he hops up on my lap and gives me a slurpy kiss that always makes me smile. Even when I get busy and forget to feed him at the exact time that he is used to being fed, he still loves me. No matter what I do, my little dog just keeps on loving me.

Did you know that God loves you that same way? There is nothing that you can do to make God stop loving you. Nothing. God's unconditional love is one of the most special gifts He has given us.

And do you know what He wants us to do with that gift? He wants us to pass it on.

What if you made your brother or sister a special present, and then you hid it away in your closet? That wouldn't bring him or her very much joy, would it?

In the same way, God wants us to share the great love that He has given to us with those around us: our neighbors across the street, the older woman who sits alone at church, even the girl who cut in front of you in line for the slide at the playground.

Today's dogs descended from wild ancestors of gray wolves.

Just like God loves us no matter what we do, God wants us to love others that same way. It is not always easy, but we don't have to do it on our own. God will be there to help us with every act of love we choose to make, big or small.

Think

Do you know someone who needs to feel God's love? What could you do to show them that love?

Journal

Write about a time when someone showed God's love to you. What did they do? How did you respond?

Pray

Dear God, thank You for Your great love. Help me to show that love to everyone I meet today, even when it is really hard to do. Amen.

a **DOLPHIN** is

**kind,
joyful,
willing to learn, and
social.**

Therefore, as God's chosen people, holy and dearly loved, clothe yourselves with compassion, kindness, humility, gentleness and patience.

Colossians 3:12

A Dolphin Is
KIND

Dolphins are aquatic mammals that live together in groups called pods. In the wild, dolphins show their kindness by helping each other. They assist other injured dolphins by helping them to the surface of the water to breathe. They also protect swimmers from sharks by swimming around the person in danger or charging at the sharks to make them go away.

Dolphins show good examples of kindness, but God is the best example of kindness. Because of God's kindness, we can have a strong, deep friendship with Him. He did not come to Earth because we deserved it; He came because of His kindness and mercy. Mercy is forgiveness we recieve when we do not deserve it.

Since God has been kind to us, we should show kindness to others. There are people around us every day who need our kindness: our family members, our friends, and other kids and adults. We all need kindness. It shows in being friendly and gentle and in showing care and concern.

Acts of kindness don't have to be hard to do. They can be as easy as giving a compliment to a friend or doing a chore without being asked. Try letting someone go ahead of you

Dolphins' clicks are some of the loudest sounds made by marine animals.

in line. Send a card to a sick friend. Talk to someone new at school. Invite someone to play with you and your friends. Share with others, especially your younger brothers and sisters. Kindness can be as easy as saying hello to everyone you see.

Sometimes being kind takes courage. When someone is surrounded by bullies just like a swimmer surrounded by sharks, it takes bravery to stand up for the person in trouble and, like the dolphin, chase the sharks away. Remember, you have Jesus to help you. Never be afraid to tell a grown-up if someone else needs help, especially if the situation is bad or dangerous.

God tells us to clothe ourselves with kindness. In the morning, put kindness on just like you put on a shirt, and you will have the right attitude to love others all day.

Think

What are the best ways to show kindness to someone you know? What are the best ways to show kindness to someone you don't know?

Journal

Write about a time when you showed kindness to someone. Include how you helped that person and how you felt afterward.

Pray

Dear God, thank You for the kindness You always show me. Help me to be aware of Your kindness and to clothe myself with kindness toward others. Amen.

You make known to me the path of life; you will fill me with joy in your presence, with eternal pleasures at your right hand.

Psalm 16:11

A Dolphin Is
JOYFUL

Dolphins always seem to be smiling. You may have seen them frolic and follow boats at sea on television, surf the waves in movies, or make friends with humans in real life. You've probably heard them chatter with happy little sounds. It certainly seems that dolphins embody happiness.

Dolphins are playful creatures, and researchers acknowledge that they are very social and seem to enjoy interaction with humans as well as dolphins. But, in truth, no creature is happy all the time ... no matter how things look.

You might be surprised to know the truth behind that dolphin smile: dolphins seem to be smiling because of their curved mouths and the physical configuration of their jaws. Their expression never really changes, no matter what their emotions. There are plenty of documented cases of dolphins who are downright grumpy and have been known to snap at people and cause trouble.

Humans sometimes act a lot like dolphins. We put on a smile when we really don't feel like it. Have you ever felt sad on the

Every dolphin makes his or her own whistle sound.

inside, but put on a happy face? It's okay. We all go through challenges that make us feel down. But faith means we can have joy even when we aren't happy.

Happiness is a temporary feeling that depends on our circumstances. Joy comes from God and is deeper and lasting. Joy is a choice that comes from an ongoing relationship with God. God's very presence can fill us with joy, and we can look forward to eternal pleasure with Him, no matter what is happening in the moment.

Next time you feel sad, don't despair. Turn to God in prayer to rediscover the joy you can have inside. That will bring a real smile to your face.

Think

When you feel sad, what do you like to do to feel better?

Journal

Draw a smiley face and a sad face, then write things that make you happy or sad under the appropriate drawing. Write about how God can help you through the harder things.

Pray

Dear God, I'm so grateful to know that I have hope in You, even when I feel sad. Please show me how to trust in You and find my joy even when things get tough. Amen.

If you are willing and obedient, you will eat the good things of the land.

Isaiah 1:19

A Dolphin Is
WILLING TO LEARN

Found in every ocean across the world, dolphins are known for their playful behavior, their intellect, and their ability to learn new commands and tricks. Without a sense of smell, and with a very limited sense of hearing, they rely on sound vibrations in the water to find the location of food, objects, and other dolphins. This type of communication is called echolocation.

In captivity, dolphins are often trained to perform. They wow audiences with their dives, flips, and quick tricks in and out of the water. They are so smart and teachable. But how do they do it?

To start, dolphins must be willing to learn. With brains similar in size to human brains, dolphins are fully capable of mastering simple skills and putting them together in a sequence. But they won't do it for just anyone. By spending time with their trainers and getting to know them, they learn to communicate with each other. A trainer listens to the dolphin's clicks, whistles, and squeaks and is able to respond. The dolphin watches the trainer's hand signals and body language and is able to build trust. When the relationship is positive, the bond is strengthened.

Dolphin clicks are produced using six air sacs near their blowholes.

This is also the way we build a relationship with the Lord. First, we must be willing to learn. By spending time with God's Word, we get to know who God is. He listens to us as we pray, and sometimes we are able to sense that He is responding. At other times, we may try to pray and no words come out. When this happens, we can be assured that the Spirit intercedes for us and God knows exactly what is on our hearts. As we communicate with the Lord, we learn to trust Him, and the bond is strengthened.

If we are willing and obedient, God will teach us all kinds of things. He is a patient teacher and we can trust that He wants good for us.

Think

Have you ever had to teach someone a new skill, like catching a ball, skipping, or tying shoes? What was difficult about the process? What was easy?

Journal

Write about a new skill that you would like to learn. Why do you want to learn it? Who would be a good person to help you?

Pray

Dear Lord, help me to be willing and obedient in all things. I want to learn and grow and become closer to You. Amen.

Offer hospitality to one another without grumbling.

1 Peter 4:9

A Dolphin Is
SOCIAL

When I think of dolphins, I remember a boat ride I took in Florida. As the boat glided along on the ocean, a couple of dolphins swam up next to us and stayed with us for the rest of the trip. It was like they had made friends with our boat!

Dolphins are very social creatures. You rarely see a dolphin alone. They swim together, eat together, and play together. They help other members of their pods, as well as swimmers and other sea creatures, when needed.

God made us to be social as well. He wants us to spend time with others, laughing, growing, eating, learning, and worshipping. Humans, like dolphins, were created to live our lives in community. Wouldn't life be boring without the company of our friends and family?

Of course, sometimes living with others can be hard, but God wants us to help others, even if it is inconvenient for us. He wants us to support one another in our challenges.

If someone is lonely, God wants us to visit with them. If someone is sick, He wants us to pray with them. If an elderly neighbor is not strong enough to do yard work, God wants us to help him out.

Each dolphin's dorsal fin is as unique as a human fingerprint.

God wants us to pray for each other, love each other, and support each other when we need a friend. God wants us to take care of the people in our community that need our help, just like the dolphins do.

Think

Who in your life would be happy if you sat and visited with them? How could that visit make them feel better?

Journal

Write about a time when you were sad or lonely, and another person helped you. What did they do? How did that make you feel?

Pray

Dear God, thank You for a heart that loves other people. Help me to remember that the greatest gift I can give someone is time spent with them. Amen.

an **ELEPHANT** is

**strong,
reliable,
pack-oriented, and
protects the weak.**

I can do all this through him who gives me strength.

Philippians 4:13

An Elephant Is
STRONG

Have you ever done something that took a lot of physical strength? Maybe you crossed from one side of the jungle gym to the other, without help from Mom or Dad. Or maybe you used your muscles to carry something really heavy during a family project. Maybe you swam for hours and hours, enjoying a hot, summer day that God had made. It feels good to be a strong and helpful person.

Animals can be strong too—amazingly strong, really. The strongest land animal in the world is the African Bull Elephant. It is well known for its incredible strength and enormous size. These beautiful creatures can carry nearly 20,000 pounds. That is like carrying five cars, or two sailboats, or forty grand pianos! God truly made the African Bull Elephant super strong.

God also makes us super strong, but not always in a physical way. Eating healthy foods and exercising can help our bodies be strong, but God can also help us be strong when we go through hard things in life.

Sometimes friendships can be hard. He's there to guide us.

If people we love become sick, He gives us the strength we need to endure.

The elephant is the largest land mammal in the world.

If something frustrating happens, like your brother or sister takes your toy and it makes you so mad, God can give you the strength to control your temper and not erupt like a volcano.

When we read the Bible and pray to God for the strength that only He can provide, we can be sure He will give us the strength we need, when we need it. When you know Jesus, you never have to go through anything all by yourself.

Think

When has God given you strength?

Journal

Do you need strength from God? Or is it easier to go through hard times by yourself?

Pray

Dear God, thank You for the strength You share with me every day. Amen.

God is faithful, who has called you into fellowship with his Son, Jesus Christ our Lord.

1 Corinthians 1:9

An Elephant Is
RELIABLE

Shirley the elephant had a long, tough life in the circus, and then lived in a zoo for over twenty years. As the only elephant at the zoo, Shirley probably longed for an elephant friend. Would you be lonely without a friend of your own?

When the zoo retired Shirley, she moved to an elephant sanctuary. There, staff members placed Shirley in a stall where she could be introduced to members of the herd as they came in for the night. One by one, she received sniffs and looks by curious elephants through the bars. As it got dark, the last elephant, Jenny, returned to the barn … and that's when things got crazy.

As soon as Jenny entered, she seemed anxious to get to Shirley. The two elephants trumpeted, swayed, chirped, roared, reached for each other with their trunks, and attempted to climb over the bars to get closer. They were so desperate to be near each other that they bent the bars separating them!

Staff members later found out that Shirley and Jenny had been in the same circus twenty-three years earlier. They remembered each other. The special bond they shared had endured.

Elephants can smell water up to three miles away.

From that moment, the two were inseparable. Shirley and Jenny had a reliable friendship, even though they had been apart for many years. Now as older elephants, the pair roamed the sanctuary together, ate together, and slept together. Shirley and Jenny could count on each other.

One of the characteristics that makes elephants so special is their memory. They don't forget things over time. Wild elephants remember the path to water, how to stay away from danger, and friends they make throughout their lives.

Can you imagine having a friend that you can count on, even after you've been separated for so long? The Bible says God loves you like that. He will never forget you. You can count on him no matter what.

God's love for you will not fade with time or space. Even when you make mistakes, God's love—like Shirley's and Jenny's—is reliable.

Think

How is God reliable in your life? Consider how He provides for your family, keeps you safe, and so on.

Journal

Write a short story about an animal friendship. Use your pets—or elephants—as the main characters. Show how the friendship is reliable.

Pray

Dear Lord, thank You for Your faithfulness to me. Help me learn how to be a reliable friend to others, just as You are to me. Amen.

*If one part suffers, every part suffers with it;
if one part is honored, every part rejoices with it.*

1 Corinthians 12:26

An Elephant Is

PACK-ORIENTED

Elephants are large land animals that travel as a herd. A herd is like a family because the group lives, eats, and moves together. Just like humans, they cuddle, race, swim dance, and even spray each other with water.

Most importantly, they take care of each other. Elephants usually stay together their whole lives, so they form incredibly close bonds with their family members. When a new baby is born, the whole herd rejoices in celebration. When one elephant is hurt or sad, the other elephants comfort it. Elephants have even been known to cry real tears!

God gives us families so that we have lifelong relationships to help us through our sad and happy times. When you are sad about the loss of a pet or a broken toy, your family can offer comfort and assurance. When it's your birthday or you receive a good grade on a test, your family can rejoice and celebrate your happiness, too.

Sometimes you may be upset with a family member. Moms, dads, siblings, and grandparents all make mistakes. If you can't talk to a family member, God is always willing to listen. He will also comfort and celebrate with you, and He can help you forgive your family members.

An elephant can lift up to 770 pounds with its trunk.

for any hurt they cause. When you cooperate and work together, your family bond will become stronger.

In an elephant herd, the mom is the leader of the family. Maybe the leader of your family is your dad or your grandmother. Some elephant herds are large and some are small. Your family may have a lot of kids, or maybe it's just you. Each family is unique and special in its own way. God loves variety and God loves you!

Think

Recall a time when a family member helped you when you were sad or celebrated with you when you were happy.

Journal

Describe a special quality about each of your family members by writing a list or drawing a picture.

Pray

Dear Lord, thank You for creating my family. I am glad to have people I can count on when I am happy or sad. Amen.

Speak up for those who cannot speak for themselves, for the rights of all who are destitute.

Proverbs 31:8

An Elephant
PROTECTS THE WEAK

Not only does a mother elephant protect her calf, but all the members of a herd work together to threaten predators and keep the small and weak members of the herd safe. The older female elephants of a herd recognize dangers ahead of time, and lead the herd toward safety. Predators are no match for a full-grown elephant who senses danger.

Everyone feels weak and needs protecting at times. Jesus tells us that He will be our protector, like a good shepherd protecting his sheep. He also tells us that He is like a strong fortress that keeps us safe inside.

Jesus also asks us to be protectors. He asks us to think about and give our attention to the weak. He asks us to speak up for those who cannot speak for themselves.

It might seem difficult to feel like a big strong elephant when you are a child, but Jesus never asks us to do something all by ourselves. Jesus says if you pay attention to the weak, He will deliver you. He is always there, helping us respond to His call.

When you see someone who needs protecting, you can pray for that person. You can also encourage them and be kind to them. If someone is in

Under water, elephants use their trunks as snorkels.

trouble, always tell your parents so they can help. You may not always know the best way to help, but an adult will be able to help you.

Sometimes people who have disabilities may need help. It's a good idea to ask them how you can help. All people like being included in fun and games. Getting to know people with disabilities and learning to appreciate their personalities, talents, and gifts is a great way to be a true defender of the weak.

The most valuable thing to give someone in need is your time. Look for ways you can include others in your activities, eat with them, share what you have, and speak up for those who cannot speak for themselves. Even as a child, you can be a powerful protector of the weak.

Think

Who do you know right now who needs protecting? What can you do to help them?

Journal

Write about a time when you felt weak. How did you see Jesus protecting you?

Pray

Dear Lord, thank You for always protecting me. Help me to see others who need me to help them and show me what to do. Amen.

a **FLAMINGO** is

**beautiful,
self-confident,
spunky, and
graceful.**

The Lord your God is with you, the Mighty Warrior who saves. He will take great delight in you; in his love he will no longer rebuke you, but will rejoice over you with singing.

Zephaniah 3:17

A Flamingo Is
BEAUTIFUL

Flamingos are fabulous, beautiful birds. God made them to stand out.

You would think they would wobble on their tall skinny legs, but they're so well balanced, they even sleep on one leg! God had a purpose for the design of those tall birds. With their long limbs standing in the water, their fluffy pink feathers seem to float above the surface while they rest.

God also had a purpose for how he made you. He knows every hair on your head, every bone in your body, every freckle on your face, every twinkle in your eyes.

You are beautiful. And it has nothing to do with the fact that you look like a movie star (or don't at all). You are beautiful because you are a child of God. Our beauty comes straight from God, who is rejoicing over us. He takes delight in us.

Humans have something extra special. When God made the world at the beginning of time, He created people in His own image. He created people to be like Him in some ways. We can think and feel, and we

Flamingos are usually pink, but they can also be red, orange, cream, or white.

understand right and wrong. So anything good in us comes from God. It reflects His own goodness.

He is the most beautiful—powerful, glorious, and wonderful.

If someone tells you that you're beautiful, that's very kind of them. Just remember that physical beauty—what you look like—is not really important. Physical beauty is not reliable, like God is. You might feel beautiful one day, and kind of icky the next.

True beauty doesn't come and go. It's not based on how you feel or how you look. Beauty is not from hair or make-up or trendy clothes (or in the case of the flamingo, fancy feathers). Real beauty is God's love and glory that shines through us, making our eyes and hearts light up and point others to Him.

Think

What are some of your favorite beautiful things in God's creation?

Journal

What does it mean to be beautiful?

Pray

Dear God, please help me to see Your glory in the beautiful things of this world. Help me to see beauty the way You do, not the way the world does. Amen.

*I praise you because I am fearfully and wonderfully made;
your works are wonderful, I know that full well.*

Psalm 139:14

A Flamingo Is
SELF-CONFIDENT

Flamingos may seem to be the most self-confident birds on the planet. As they stand tall with their bright, bold, and beautiful pink feathers, they easily catch our attention. But really, flamingos are just being who God created them to be.

The pink color of a flamingo comes from the beta-carotene in the food they eat, which is mostly algae, shrimp, plants, and bugs. We eat foods with beta-carotene, too. Vegetables like carrots and spinach have lots of beta-carotene, which means that if we eat enough of them (like every day, at every meal, for the rest of our lives) our skin could potentially turn shades of orange or green. Wouldn't that be cool?

But God designed us to eat more than just carrots and spinach. He didn't want us to all look the same. In fact, he created humans to be all shapes and sizes, with all types of hair and all colors of skin. Do you think that penguins, with their short, chubby legs, look at flamingos and feel jealous of their long, slender ones? No way! Penguins were given the exact body size and shape they need to waddle on the ground and swim in the sea. They don't need the

The legs of an adult flamingo are longer than its body.

long legs of a flamingo that help them balance while they are hunting for food and are lightweight enough to help them take flight quickly.

It's easy for us to compare our bodies with those of our friends. Girls with curly hair may want straight hair. Boys with skinny arms may want more muscles. But it's important to remember that God created each of us in His own image and we are each "fearfully and wonderfully made."

God does not make mistakes in His design of creation—not with the penguins, not with the flamingos, and not with us. We can be confident in who we are when we remember who made us.

Think

Choose a characteristic (physical or not) that you like most about yourself.

Journal

We may look at our hair, body, or skin to determine our worth, but God looks at our heart. Write down three non-physical characteristics of yourself that God would be proud of.

Pray

Dear Lord, help me to keep my confidence in You. I know that you gave me this body, this brain, and this heart for a purpose. I put my trust in You. Amen.

In the same way, let your light shine before others, that they may see your good deeds and glorify your Father in heaven.

Matthew 5:16

A Flamingo Is

SPUNKY

God was pretty creative when He made animals, wasn't he? He only made one that is covered in pink feathers, stands on one leg, and eats with its head upside down. What would people say if we dressed up in pink feathers and stood on one leg? I bet they would say we were pretty spunky.

"Spunky" is kind of a funny-sounding word. It means having a lot of spirit and courage. It means being determined and brave. One of my favorite ways to be spunky is to not be afraid to show my love for God. Sometimes it is easy to share God's love with others, like when we are at Sunday school or church camp. Other times, it is more difficult, like when we bow our heads to pray in a restaurant and other people do not. That can feel uncomfortable and strange.

God loves us all and gave us a special desire to love Him, deep in our hearts. God wants us to share His love with everyone in our world. Sometimes that is not easy. In fact, sometimes it is just plain hard to do.

It helps to remember that by loving others, we might bring them to know our Savior, Jesus Christ. What if, by our

Flamingos adapt well to both cold and warm climates.

showing God's love to others, they learned about God's great and unfailing love for them?

Shine your own spunky light. Show God's love to everyone you meet. Like the bright pink feathers of our flamingo friends, let people see your love for God. May your spunky display of love inspire others to know God's great love for them.

Think

When is it easy for you to share God's love? When is it uncomfortable?

Journal

Write about a time when you shared God's love. What did you do? How did it make you feel? How do you think it made others feel?

Pray

Dear God, thank You for loving me so much. Help me to share Your love every day to help make our world a better place. Amen.

With great power the apostles continued to testify to the resurrection of the Lord Jesus. And God's grace was so powerfully at work in them all that there were no needy persons among them.

Acts 4:33-34

A Flamingo Is
GRACEFUL

Flamingos are some of the most graceful birds in creation. The way they balance on one leg reminds me of the posture of a prima ballerina. Add in the sophisticated curve of their necks and the feathers that call tutus to mind, and flamingos are the picture of elegance.

Really, though, flamingos aren't ballerinas. They're just flamingos being flamingos!

You are a graceful creature, too, because you are exactly who God made *you* to be.

We often use the word "graceful" to describe someone who makes swift, fluid movements, or to mean the opposite of clumsy. But when we think in terms of faith, to be full of grace (or graceful) is to be filled with God. Grace is how we see God acting in our lives. It's how He loves us, forgives us, provides for us, and shares Himself with us. It's abundant, and it's more than we deserve. Grace is a beautiful gift.

We move with grace when we open our hearts to His word and His will for us. Keeping our hearts close to His means that we can live balanced lives, too. We will do beautiful things, because we are filled with God and His love. And what we do

In the wild, a flamingo colony can contain thousands of birds.

will attract others to God, too. When we live the way we were created to live—in union with God and trusting in His love—then we testify to the Resurrection. That may sound like a tough thing to do, but really, it's exactly what we were created to do.

A simple yes on our part to be open to and accepting of God's grace will allow Him to be powerfully at work in us, just like He was in the Apostles after the Resurrection. And just like He is in flamingos being flamingos today!

Think

How have you experienced God active in your life?

Journal

When do you feel closest to God? How might He be using that to draw you and others closer to Himself?

Pray

Dear God, help me to open my heart to You, so that You can fill it with Your grace. Amen.

a **FOX** is

quick,
curious, and
clever.

He says, "Be still, and know that I am God; I will be exalted among the nations, I will be exalted in the earth."

Psalm 46:10

A Fox Is
QUICK

Foxes dart across the grassy fields to forage for food, dash over rocky hillsides to seek out homes to rest their heads, and bolt through lush forests to investigate what their neighbors are doing. Foxes are busy, and they are quick! They speed in and speed out of almost everywhere they go. Their camouflaged coats and speedy paws carry them from here to there, lickety-split.

Maybe sometimes you dart from one thing to the next like a fox. Being a part of many things can be fun, but sometimes you miss the blessings around you if you move too quickly. Imagine you had soccer practice, went to your friend's house, worked on homework, ate dinner, took a bath, and now you want to play one last quick video game. But your little brother wants you to play cars with him. How do you decide what to do?

It's easy to forget what's important when you're busy rushing from one thing to the next. But the good news is, God wants to help us learn how to balance the quickness of life, so we can make the most out of our time with Him and with our friends and family. We don't have to fill our lives like quick little foxes dashing across a field in a blur. That might not really make us happy in the end anyway.

Fox tracks can be identified by four oval toe imprints in front of a chevron-shaped heel pad.

Whatever you are doing today, take a step away to see little moments God is sharing with you to bring you joy. It could be reading your sister a book, going to a friend's soccer game, playing a card game with your grandma, making a batch of cookies and sharing with your neighbor, or sitting on a grassy hillside to watch a quick fox dash back and forth from its den.

When you do, you'll see that even the quick fox slows down, looks around to enjoy the surrounding beauty, and snuggles up with its kits to enjoy some together time.

Think

How do we know God likes us to spend time with Him?

Journal

Describe a time when you really wanted to do something on your own, but ended up spending time with someone instead.

Pray

Dear Lord, thank You for the time I get to spend together with You, my family, and my friends. Please help me to slow down and see You in the people closest to me. Amen.

The heart of the discerning acquires knowledge, for the ears of the wise seek it out.

Proverbs 18:15

A Fox Is
CURIOUS

Foxes have extremely good senses. They can hear a mouse scratching around under the ground. They can follow the scent of a small animal for long distances. They can see a sparrow zip across a fallen branch.

When a fox hears a tiny rustle of dry leaves, it becomes curious. What is making that noise? Where is it? Where is it going? Could it be something good to eat?

If a fox smells another fox nearby, it wants to know who it is. Is it a mate? One of its kits? Or is it a strange fox trying to move into its territory? The fox follows the scent from bush to bush, tree to tree until its curiosity is satisfied.

Foxes also have super-duper vision. Their special eyes can change from day vision to night vision. If a tiny lizard skitters in front of it, a fox can see it whether it's day or night. And, of course, this makes the fox curious. It wants to know where the critter is going and whether or not it will make a tasty snack.

When a fox sees, smells, or hears something unusual, it wants to know what it is, where it is, and why it is there. The fox is curious—it wants to know more.

Foxes use their dens to store extra food.

Kids can be curious, too. Do you ever wonder how things work? Or do you wonder why people act as they do? Or why some things are good and some things are bad? And when you wonder, do you want to find the answers like foxes do? Do you go "sniffing around" until you learn where or why or how?

Scripture tells us that those with curious hearts and minds acquire knowledge. Those who are wise search for it. Curiosity is what makes people look for answers to questions big and small. All inventions and discoveries start with curiosity.

Are you seeking and searching for new things to learn? If so, that means you are curious. Good for you!

Are you curious about God? Do you want to learn more about Him? Understand Him better? The Bible also tells us we will find God when we seek Him with all our hearts. Start seeking. You'll find your answers in time.

Think

What is something that you are really curious about?

Journal

Write about something new you've learned recently. What made you curious about it? Where and how did you learn more about the subject?

Pray

Dear Lord, this universe that You made is filled with mysteries. Make me want to learn about all the things and people in this wide, wonderful world that You created. Amen.

If any of you lacks wisdom, you should ask God, who gives generously to all without finding fault, and it will be given to you.

James 1:5

A Fox Is
CLEVER

Have you ever heard the phrase "clever as a fox"?

"Clever" is another word for smart or intelligent. Throughout history, foxes have been described as clever because of their ability to find food, trick their predators, and get themselves out of sticky situations. As members of the canine family, they are similar to wolves or dogs. They are also known to be fast and light on their feet.

All of this serves them well for survival in the wild, but in fairytales and folklore, the fox often has a bad reputation. Being solitary animals, foxes often live on their own. With no one to look after but themselves, their cleverness is self-seeking. Foxes are omnivores—they eat meat and plants—and they will eat absolutely anything. Their desire for more often leads to sneaky behavior.

God created foxes to be clever, because He knew they would need a certain slyness to survive in the wild. Their "street smarts" keep them fed and alert to danger.

God created us to be clever as well, but then He went one step further and created us to be wise. If cleverness is knowing how to get out of a difficult situation, then wisdom is knowing how to avoid the troublesome spot altogether. Doesn't that sound like a better idea?

Foxes have such sensitive ears that if a fox hears an animal underground, it can dig it up and catch it.

By reading the Bible, praying, and being an active part of our church communities, we begin to understand the difference between right and wrong, allowing us to make good choices as we grow up. If we get stuck and don't know which way to go, the Bible tells us to "ask God, who gives generously to all."

Thankfully, we don't have to live life on our own, like foxes. We don't have to have all the answers, and we surely don't have to be sneaky, because God provides what we need. When we put our faith and hope in Jesus, we can be clever and wise at the same time.

Think

Give a real-life example of being clever versus being wise. How are they the same? How are they different?

Journal

Write about a time when you were clever. How did your cleverness serve you? What did you gain from it?

Pray

Dear Lord, thank You for not leaving me to figure out life on my own. Help me to make good choices as I grow, to be both clever and wise. Amen.

a HIPPOPOTAMUS is

protective,

independent,

aggressive, and

lives in community.

*God is our refuge and strength,
an ever-present help in trouble.*

Psalm 46:1

A Hippo Is
PROTECTIVE

Hippopotamuses, or hippos for short, are the third largest living mammal (only elephants and white rhinos are bigger). Hippos can weigh anywhere from 2,900 to 4,000 pounds.

While they don't look very scary, don't be fooled. They are just as dangerous as lions and wolves. A hippo can bite with the force of 2,000 pounds per square inch! Sure, they may only eat plants and never hunt other animals, but if they feel threatened, they will attack.

Hippos are fierce protectors of each other and of their young. They travel in herds because the group offers protection against predators who might attack a single hippo, but who will run away from a herd of hippos. You might say that hippos look out for each other. They've got each other's backs.

You know who has your back? God! That's right; the Creator of the universe has your back. He is your protector. The Bible tells us that God will never leave us. No matter how alone you might feel at times, remember that God is always with you.

The Bible also says that God will be your shelter in times of trouble.

Hippos can run faster than humans.

He will surround you with His protection, just like the herd of hippos surrounds the baby hippos in order to keep them from any danger. You can trust God, and you can be at peace knowing that He is watching over you. He is your Heavenly Father and your constant protector. And, just like an adult hippo, God will defend His children (that's you!) no matter what.

Think

Just because you can't see God doesn't mean He isn't with you. Name some other examples of things you can't see, yet are powerful (for example, the wind).

Journal

Write about a time when God protected you from something dangerous or threatening. Did you take time to thank Him? If not, write a thank-you prayer to God right now.

Pray

Dear God, thank You for watching over me, for protecting me, and for promising to never leave me. Amen.

And so we know and rely on the love God has for us. God is love. Whoever lives in love lives in God, and God in them.

1 John 4:16

A Hippo Is
INDEPENDENT

Hippos are sometimes seen soaking in cool rivers or sleeping on sandy beaches by the water's edge all alone. Even though hippos appear very independent, they are known to have the biggest hearts in the animal kingdom. They are very loving and caring animals, always concerned about their hippo family's and friends' well-being. Hippos don't have to worry that they don't have someone to lean on, even if they seem to be alone. Hippos know their family and friends are always there for them.

Have you ever felt like you're all alone, even if you have a lot of friends, family, and people who care about you? Wouldn't it be nice to know someone is always there for you?

Feeling like you are alone with nowhere to go can happen, but you're never alone when you have God. He's the help that's there to guide you, the friend who will listen, and the family who will care for you, like the hippos care for each other. God asks us to rely on Him to walk us through the moments that seem too big for us to handle on our own. He helps us feel

"Hippopotamus" means "river horse."

better when we're lonely, scared, or sad. God asks us to rely on his love.

Whatever you are doing today may have you feeling like you're the one and only hippo soaking in a cool river all by yourself, but you're not alone. God is with you wherever you go and in whatever you do. It's okay to have days that make you feel like there's no one out there for you, because these are the times when you can call on God.

You can depend on Him and remember that the things that are impossible with men are possible with God. You can rely on Him to surround you with His love, and to provide family and friends who will be there for you, just like the hippos are there for each other.

Think

Remember a time when you helped a friend or family member know that you're there for them.

Journal

Write about a time when you were there for a friend, just like a hippo is for its friends.

Pray

Dear Lord, thank You for being there for me when I feel alone. Please help me to be a light for others, so they know they can rely on You. Amen.

But the fruit of the Spirit is love, joy, peace, forbearance, kindness, goodness, faithfulness, gentleness and self-control.

Galatians 5:22-23

A Hippo Is
AGGRESSIVE

You might say that hippopotamuses are like giant gray pigs that love to swim in the water. They have big, toothy grins; tiny tails; and little ears that always seem to be moving. These features, along with their constant smiles, make hippos adorable!

But hippos are also one of the most dangerous animals in the world. That's because they're so aggressive, meaning they're quick to pick a fight. The males who are in charge fight predators to protect the females and babies, which is a good thing. But they also fight each other over territory and family disputes, and it doesn't take much to get them riled up. When people get too close to hippos in the wild, they can get seriously hurt.

You know what hippos remind me of? Bullies—kids who act really sweet in front of a teacher, but then are mean to the other kids when the teacher isn't looking. Being aggressive with other kids is hurtful and wrong.

The Bible tells us that it's okay to feel angry sometimes, but we should never act out by fighting or saying ugly things to people. Instead, we should try to be more like Jesus: gentle, patient, good, and kind. Sometimes, it's harder to be nice than it is to be

A group of hippos may be known as a herd, a pod, or a bloat.

mean. But if we pray for God's help, He'll give us the strength we need to be kind.

You can practice being gentle and kind wherever you are! If your little sister breaks your toy, forgive her instead of yelling at her. If a new kid comes to school, welcome him by being friendly and sitting next to him in class or at lunch. Make sure you don't pick on other kids who have health problems, wear unusual clothes, or act differently than you do. Instead, treat them the way you want to be treated.

If you see someone being picked on, teased, or laughed at, tell an adult so she can put a stop to it.

Hippos look really sweet, but they don't always act that way. Instead of being aggressive like a hippo, make a point to be kind and gentle. This way, you're sure to make new friends, and you'll make God happy, too!

Think

Who can you tell if you see someone being bullied or if you're bullied by another kid?

Journal

Write about a time when you saw someone else being bullied. How do you think he or she felt?

Pray

Dear God, please forgive me for when I've been aggressive with or bullied anyone. Help me to be kind and gentle and an example of Your love. Amen.

How good and pleasant it is when God's people live together in unity!

Psalm 133:1

A Hippo
LIVES IN COMMUNITY

Hippos are herd animals, which means they live in groups. Together, they protect their young, swim, and search for food. People have groups they are a part of, too, called communities.

Communities are more than just people living in the same area. Communities are made up of people we can rely on for friendship and encouragement when times are tough. They give us a sense of belonging and purpose. By connecting with people through a common bond, you can feel the difference you are making in the world and that you are part of something special. God gave us communities so we wouldn't be alone.

Chances are, you belong to several communities. They might be through a church, a school, an activity, or a town. What makes your community a special place to be a part of? Do you share the same beliefs or similar interests? Does being a member bring you joy?

When individuals come together to form communities, God rejoices in their peace and shared happiness. As a member of a community, you have a very important job: to be a good member. Just as a community

Hippos rest in water or mud during the day and come on land at sunset to eat plants.

is there for you, you need to be there for it, too. And you don't need to be as big as a hippo to help; even the smallest members can make a real impact.

Take a walk with your family and collect litter to help keep your community beautiful. If a friend in your community is feeling sad, take time to listen to her feelings and offer her encouragement. Prepare hot meals for members of your community when they are sick. Reaching out to those in need and doing your part when work needs to be done will help your community thrive and prosper, and you will feel a sense of pride and accomplishment for being a part of something special. Be good to your community and your community will be good to you.

The next time you're feeling under the weather or bluer than the ocean, a member of your community may return the favor and do something special for you!

Think

What communities do you belong to and what ties each together?

Journal

hink of two actions you can take to help your community.

Pray

Dear Lord, I am thankful for my community. Please help me to be a faithful member, who befriends the lonely, cares for the sick, feeds the hungry, and spreads joy. Amen.

a LION is

a leader,

courageous,

brave, and

just.

Then one of the elders said to me, "Do not weep! See, the Lion of the tribe of Judah, the Root of David, has triumphed. He is able to open the scroll and its seven seals."

Revelation 5:5

A Lion Is a
LEADER

Imagine the bright sun, sitting in a clear, blue sky. Imagine tall, brown grass, swaying in an afternoon breeze. Now, what if, crouched in that grass, lay a thick, bushy mane attached to a set of piercing eyes and a strong jaw, with sharp teeth, ready to pounce at any moment?

Do you know which animal this describes?

Yes, that's right, a lion!

Lions are such majestic creatures. They're known as the King of the Jungle. Male lions protect their prides, or groups of lions, territory, and cubs. They are not afraid to frighten away intruders. Female lions, also known as lionesses, are incredible hunters. It is a lioness's duty to feed the pride. Both male and female lions are strong, powerful animals.

You may already know that Jesus is the Lamb of God, but did you know that He is also known as the Lion of Judah? Once you understand that Jesus died for your sins and you put Him in your heart as a Christian, you have Jesus as your protector and guardian. He is the strongest and the most powerful, and He is watching over you, like the lions who guard their prides.

Lions live in groups called prides.

What a beautiful and comforting thought this is! Jesus, who knows all, who created the moon and the stars, loves you so much that He protects you. He guides you. He wants the very best for you.

With Jesus, the Lion of Judah, by our sides, we have the strength we need for whatever obstacles we face, like making choices we know will please Jesus, and helping others even when it's hard.

There's a name for people who do these things. They are called leaders. Leaders don't always think about themselves. Instead, they think about how they can help others.

Sometimes, it can be really tough to be kind, to stand up for others, and to do the things that God expects us to do. But just remember, you're never doing these things alone. You have Jesus, the ultimate leader, walking alongside you, roaring like a lion!

Think

Have you ever stood up for someone? Was it hard? How did you find the strength to do it?

Journal

How do you feel about doing hard things, knowing that Jesus is with you always?

Pray

Dear Lord, thank You for Your example. Please give me the strength and guidance I need to be the kind of leader that pleases You. Amen.

Have I not commanded you? Be strong and courageous. Do not be afraid; do not be discouraged, for the Lord your God will be with you wherever you go.

Joshua 1:9

A Lion Is
COURAGEOUS

We call Jesus a lot of different names to help describe how amazing He is. Names like Emmanuel, Son of God, Light of the World, and Savior are just a few we use when we talk to Jesus in prayer or worship. In Holy Scripture, He is often referred to as the Lion of Judah, which reminds us that He is powerful. Jesus is the King of Kings.

The Bible tells us to be courageous and not to be afraid. God is always with us. That's what one of those other names for Jesus means: "Emmanuel," or "God with us." Even though we can't see Him, it's like we are always walking with a lion beside us, and nothing can separate us from Him. Think about what it would be like to have such an amazing animal with you, protecting you, loving you.

Jesus is with us at the top of the Ferris wheel and when we are busy helping with chores. He's with us during our dentist appointments and when we meet a new friend. Sometimes, it can be hard to speak up and introduce yourself, to include someone who usually gets left out in a game, or to tell a coach that you can't make it to practice, but these are the right things to do.

A lion's roar can be heard as far as five miles away.

Doing what is right even when it is hard takes courage when you're little. It takes courage when you're big, too. It's like a lion-sized muscle that we need to exercise to be strong. Thankfully, we don't have to rely upon ourselves. One of the amazing things about Jesus is the more time we spend with Him, the more we become like Him. It's a beautiful thing! By getting to know our Lord, we become peacemakers, full of love and joy. We also become courageous like the lion.

Our courage comes from the Lord. When we remember the cross and how Jesus faced it for us, we gain the courage of a lion to do the right thing … even when it's scary.

Think

How can you practice being courageous at school, at home, or in your neighborhood?

Journal

Write about or draw someone you think is courageous. What do they do that shows courage?

Pray

Dear God, thank You for always being with me. Help me to always do what is right, even when it might be difficult. Amen.

*When you lie down, you will not be afraid;
when you lie down, your sleep will be sweet.*

Proverbs 3:24

A Lion Is
BRAVE

You don't earn the nickname "King of the Jungle" by being a cowardly animal. No, that name is reserved for a brave, bold, taking-care-of business kind of animal—the lion. While it's true the lion is one of the bravest creatures in all the animal kingdom, it's not really King of the *Jungle* because lions don't live in the jungle. Lions mostly live in the grassy savannahs of Sub-Saharan Africa. Still, they are king when it comes to hunting and defending their territory. They will fight and kill animals meaner, larger, and faster, such as warthogs, antelopes, zebras, cheetahs, leopards, and hyenas.

Maybe lions are able to hunt and defend so effectively because they are so well rested. Some experts estimate that lions sleep up to twenty hours a day. Who knew that lions were such major nappers? Or maybe lions are able to sleep so peacefully (and so many hours) because they possess that King-of-the-Jungle attitude. In other words, maybe they are able to sleep so much because they aren't afraid. They can rest without any fears or worries.

Guess what? We can do the same. We can go to sleep with confidence, knowing that we are strong, brave, and loved by almighty God.

Lions use teamwork to hunt their prey.

Lions are also able to rest well because they know if an enemy tries to attack, they have their entire lion family, also known as their pride, to back them up. Lions stick together and defend one another. God does the same for us! So, like a lion, we can rest well, knowing that God will take care of us and defend us no matter what.

You can go through life with that King-of-the-Jungle attitude, because God has made you brave, strong, bold, and confident. And He will be your protector, because He is even braver and more awesome than the King of the Jungle. He is the King of Kings!

Think

Consider the expression, "Do it afraid." With God you can "do it afraid" because He will give you strength. What is something that makes you afraid?

Journal

Write about a time when you felt nervous or afraid.

Pray

Dear God, thank You for making me brave and helping me face my fears by being my protector. Help me to be even braver and bolder—just like a lion. Amen.

He has shown you, O mortal, what is good. And what does the Lord require of you? To act justly and to love mercy and to walk humbly with your God.

Micah 6:8

A Lion Is
JUST

Lions are powerful animals. Male lions are among the biggest cats in the feline family (only the tiger is slightly bigger). They also have the loudest roar. It lets other animals and lions outside the pride know they should stay away. A male lion's mane makes him look regal and majestic, and both adult male and female lions have few natural predators.

Lions have often been used as symbols of royalty, strength, power, and justice throughout history because of their size and power. One of the most famous lions in literature is Aslan, the King of Narnia in The Chronicles of Narnia by C.S. Lewis. In *The Lion, the Witch and the Wardrobe*, the talking beasts of Narnia have been waiting for Aslan to return to defeat the White Witch and break the spell that holds their world in endless winter. C.S. Lewis created Aslan to represent Jesus, who in the Book of Revelation is called the Lion of Judah. (The world "aslan" is Turkish for "lion.")

But Jesus is not called the Lion of Judah because he has a great big roar or a huge ring of fur around his neck. Jesus is the Lion of Judah because he is all the things that lions are—strong, powerful, majestic, beautiful, fierce, loving,

Lions spend between sixteen and twenty hours each day sleeping or resting.

and so much more! Jesus is kind, full of mercy, and just, meaning he always judges fairly.

Without Jesus, you and I can never be completely good. But with Jesus living in our hearts, we have all the help we need to be fair, merciful, and kind as we live for Him in this world. That doesn't mean you will always get it right, but if you take time to talk to Him, Jesus will help you be fair to your friends, kind to your brothers and sisters, and respectful and loving to your parents.

Lions living in the African savannah must hunt, mark their territories, and protect their prides in order to survive. In order to be salt and light in this world, as Christ's followers, we must practice justice and kindness and offer grace to everyone God places in our lives. That might sound tough, but never fear: Jesus, the Lion of Judah, is with you, giving you all the power and strength you need.

Think

A person who is "just" is someone known for making fair decisions, no matter who is involved. Name someone in your life who is just and explain why.

Journal

Write about a time when you had to practice justice (in other words, be fair) to a friend or someone in your community. Were you tempted to make a different choice?

Pray

Dear Lord, sometimes it's hard to be fair. Please help me to always practice justice and make good choices, as I learn each day to be more like You. Amen.

an **OCTOPUS** is

**intelligent,
perceptive, and
flexible.**

For the Lord gives wisdom; from his mouth come knowledge and understanding.

Proverbs 2:6

An Octopus Is
INTELLIGENT

The octopus is the most intelligent invertebrate. Invertebrate is a long word for an animal that doesn't have bones. An octopus has all kinds of fun squishy parts, but none of them is a bone. The octopus is so smart, it's even more intelligent than many vertebrates, or animals that do have bones.

Octopuses are clever enough to work through mazes and figure out how to open jars, particularly if there is something tasty inside. They can squeeze their big squishy bodies through openings no bigger than their eyeballs. Octopuses can change their skin color and texture to match their environments, making them almost impossible to spot. They've been found climbing aboard fishing boats and eating the clams and other bait. And they often figure out how to escape from their aquariums.

An octopus has one big brain in its head and a smaller brain in each one of its tentacles. That's nine brains! No wonder it can learn new skills, have a memory, and even use tools. The veined octopus gathers coconut shells and uses them as armor and for its house. It even takes the coconuts along when travelling. Octopuses are amazing.

Just like fish, octopuses use gills to breathe.

As amazing as octopuses are, you are even more incredible. God created you as the most intelligent creature on our planet. Your brain is astounding! God created you to have opinions, to make choices, to solve problems, and to make beautiful things. You can sing a song, hop on one foot, and make a sandwich—all at the same time.

God loved creating the octopus, but He loved creating you even more. You and your brain are the very best of what God made. The more you grow and learn, the more intelligent you will be. When you were a baby, you couldn't talk or read. But you can talk now and are probably learning how to read more and more each day. The more you teach your brain, the smarter you will be. There is no limit to how much you can learn.

The very best thing you can do with your brain is learn about God and follow Him throughout your life. God loves it when we use our brains to do amazing things, but He loves it even more when we use our brains to love Him.

Think

Have you ever felt like you weren't very intelligent? How do you know that this is simply not true?

Journal

What are some cool things you know or know how to do? What is something new you would like to learn about this week?

Pray

Dear God, thank You for giving me such an incredible brain. Help me to use my intelligence to honor and glorify You. Amen.

To the discerning all of [my words] are right; they are upright to those who have found knowledge.

Proverbs 8:9

An Octopus Is
PERCEPTIVE

Octopuses—or, octopi, if you prefer—might be the cleverest creatures God made. They easily solve puzzles and mazes. They are perceptive detectives, which means they can take in a lot of information and use it to plot out how to fix pesky problems. Hide its food in a jar, and the octopus will learn how to unscrew the lid to get it.

One way an octopus senses its surroundings is through its skin, which can "see" light. Another way is through the suckers on its tentacles. On each of the eight tentacles of an adult Pacific octopus, there are about 280 suckers. That's a total 2,240 suckers, every one of which senses smells and flavors. Can you imagine being able to taste 2,240 ice cream cones all at once?

Octopuses have pulled off some amazing feats by putting their senses to use. An octopus named Inky escaped from the National Aquarium of New Zealand by squeezing his squishy body through a teeny gap in the lid of his tank. He slithered thirteen feet across the aquarium's deck floor. He worked the cover off a six-inch wide drainpipe. Then he oozed down the pipe to the Pacific Ocean that he sensed about 160 feet below.

Otto, a bored octopus in a German aquarium, learned that if he squirted water onto the light above his tank, he would short-circuit all

The common Atlantic octopus can change the color of its skin instantly.

the lights in the building. Otto also juggled hermit crabs, tossed rocks at his tank glass, and redecorated his home by moving everything in his tank.

At the Santa Monica Pier Aquarium in California, an octopus without any tools disassembled a valve at the top of her tank. Two hundred gallons of water overflowed onto the aquarium floor.

If octopuses could read (and maybe they can), my guess is that they would curl all eight tentacles around the Book of Proverbs. That's the book in the Bible that's full of wise sayings. Proverbs shows us that it's not enough just to know things. We are called to take the information in God's Word and let it fire up all our spiritual senses so that we understand it and can use it to glorify God. If you're as perceptive as an octopus, you won't be tricked into doing something God doesn't like.

Let's ask God to help us become perceptive detectives like the octopus.

Think

How can you become more perceptive? What kinds of training can you exercise to learn more about God's wisdom in your life?

Journal

Write about a time when you had to use perception to solve a problem. How did you piece the clues together?

Pray

Dear God, thank You for all the wonderful things You have taught me. Help me to have the wisdom to figure out the right things that You want me to do. Amen.

There is a time for everything, and a season for every activity under the heavens.

Ecclesiastes 3:1

An Octopus Is
FLEXIBLE

Octopuses are the ninjas of the sea. They can change their color to blend in with their surroundings and they are invertebrates, which means they don't have a spine. These natural gymnasts are so flexible, they can squeeze into tiny crevices to hide from predators.

For humans, being flexible isn't just about being super bendy. Flexible has another meaning—it's also an attitude. Have you ever made plans that you were excited about, then suddenly those plans changed or were cancelled altogether? Maybe rain clouds spoiled your day at the beach, or your best friend caught a cold and your playdate was cancelled.

When that happens, you might feel sad or even angry and think that it's not fair. But God tells us there is a time for everything and to be patient and trust in His plans.

Feeling a deep sense of disappointment isn't easy, but rather than dwell on those feelings, we can choose to be patient and flexible. There is joy to be found in a rainy day, even when your beach plans are cancelled. Think about what rain means to the world. Water is life for creatures big and small. Rainwater nourishes plants and helps them grow big and strong. Be flexible and commit to enjoying God's gift

Octopuses have three hearts.

of rain. Break out your rain boots and stomp in puddles. When lightning comes and thunder crashes, snuggle up with family and play your favorite board games.

Trust in God's timing. Maybe your day didn't turn out the way you had hoped, but when you're feeling discouraged, give your feelings and burden to God. Let Him guide you, and trust that He has a plan for you.

Another way you can be flexible is to compromise. A compromise is when two people disagree about something, and instead of only one person getting what he wants, both sides get a piece of their goal. If you and your sibling can't agree on what activity to do on your day off from school, do not fight or become angry with each other. Instead, find common ground and choose an activity you both enjoy. It may not be the first choice for either of you, but this way, no one is left out and everyone has a chance to enjoy the day.

Think

How can you help others be flexible and learn about compromise? Think of two or three fun activities you can do at home if a day out gets cancelled.

Journal

Write about a time when your plans were cancelled. How were you flexible and still able to have a good day?

Pray

Dear Lord, when my plans have to change, surround me with Your love. Give me flexibility, so that I can grow more resilient and stronger in faith. Amen.

an OTTER is

**friendly,
energetic,
playful, and
creative.**

Therefore encourage one another and build each other up, just as in fact you are doing.

1 Thessalonians 5:11

An Otter Is
FRIENDLY

At the zoo, I love to see all the wonderful and interesting animals God has made. In a special way, I enjoy the otters. Otters live in large groups, which are called "rafts" when they are at rest and "romps" when they are active. Otters are known to be playful. They slide down hills and splash in the water. You might even catch an otter "juggling rocks."

It's funny to think of an otter being friendly. Many times, we might not think much of our friendships. We get so used to playing with our friends, but to God, our friendships are very important. He places special people in our lives, so we can love and encourage one another.

To encourage someone can mean offering a kind word when a friend is having a stressful or sad day. It might be telling a friend not to quit when frustrated with a sport or a school subject. It may even be letting a lonely friend know how much you and God care.

It is a real privilege, or gift, to have a friend. God is so good to us that He gives us these lovely friendships. You know that Jesus died for you on the cross, but have you ever thought that Jesus died for your friends, too? Yes, He absolutely did! He loves you and your friends so much that He died for all of you (and me)!

Sea otters have the densest fur of any animal.

The truth is, Jesus expects us to love our friends like He does.

I bet you've had fun times with your friends just like the friendly otter has, splashing and being silly. Thank God for the special people He has given you. Ask Him to help you love and encourage them!

Think

When have you encouraged a friend? When has a friend encouraged you?

Journal

Draw a picture of you and your friends playing.

Pray

Dear God, thank You for the friends You've given me. Help me to please You and to appreciate my friends. Amen.

Whatever you do, work at it with all your heart, as working for the Lord, not for human masters, since you know that you will receive an inheritance from the Lord as a reward.

Colossians 3:23-24

An Otter Is
ENERGETIC

Otters love to play. They slide down sand banks. They dive into the water. They play chase and tag and dive for shells. But otters are also often busy finding food and taking care of their little otters. They are high-energy creatures. When they've played themselves out, or worked until they are tired, they know to lay back in the water and float to rest up.

Are you high-energy when it's time to play basketball or soccer? Do you ride your bike or play hide-and-seek until you are worn out? Jumping on a trampoline or chasing a Frisbee can really make you tired, too. Those things take lots of energy, but they are worth it because they are so much fun.

Do you feel the same way about raking the yard or putting away your laundry? Or do you drag through your chores? They are not exactly fun, are they? But God's Word tells us that we are not to be motivated by fun. Lots of things we need to do are not fun. We should do every job (even those that aren't fun) with all our hearts and all our energy to please the Lord.

If we didn't do laundry, we would have nothing to wear. If we didn't do dishes, we would be eating off dirty plates. Yuck! What if no one mowed the lawn or raked the leaves?

River otters are smaller than sea otters.

When your enthusiasm for a chore is sluggish, try this trick: Pretend you are making your bed to please God. Put away the dishes as if Jesus were standing nearby, watching. You wouldn't want God to sleep in a messy bed, or Jesus to search all over the kitchen to find a cereal bowl, would you?

The opposite of working with energy is laziness. Spending lots of time stretched out in bed or on the sofa with a tablet or cell phone isn't energetic. I can't imagine an otter doing that!

Choose to do the opposite. Keep your mind energetic with books. Keep your body energetic by playing outside and being on sports teams. Keep your heart energetic by doing things for others and for God.

Stay busy when it's time to be busy. Rest when it's time to rest. These things are sure to please the Lord.

Think

What are some things you can do to feel more energetic and enthusiastic about a not-so-fun task?

Journal

Think of a task you've been putting off and why you haven't started it. Promise yourself that you will finish it by a certain date. When you do, celebrate with a giant star on your page!

Pray

Dear Lord, help me to do everything with energy and enthusiasm. Keep me from laziness, so that I can work hard and do every job with my best ability. Amen.

*So whether you eat drink or whatever you do,
do it all for the glory of God.*

1 Corinthians 10:31

An Otter Is
PLAYFUL

Fun, furry aquatic mammals, otters are members of the weasel family. They have short legs and webbed feet, which make them excellent swimmers. Playful otters can put a smile on anyone's face. Otters love to drop to their bellies and slide along the water's edge. Although it is a great way to get from one spot to another, otters clearly enjoy themselves, and they will slide over and over just for fun.

Like otters, children enjoy playing. Play brings joy and happiness. But sometimes we may wonder if God wants us to have fun. What does God think about playing?

We know that God is holy and that He expects us to do what the Bible says. We also know that He loves us and wants us to love others. God tells us to be glad, and that a merry heart is good for us. In fact, He is the one who gives us hearts that enjoy playtime with our friends and loved ones.

Otters are playful and lighthearted. When you are playful, you also have a happy heart and a cheerful face. God does not want us to have a crushed spirit, which is when your heart aches and you cannot find any hope. God made playtime as one way to have a happy heart.

Sea otters spend hours each day caring for their fur, to be sure it can trap enough air and keep them warm and dry.

It brings God joy if when we play, we honor Him in the way we play. Are we kind and do we share our toys? Do we follow the rules of the games that we play and treat others with love and respect? Playing brings us happiness, but true happiness comes from God when we honor Him in all things, even in our play time.

Although God has created us to enjoy fun and playing, He does not want us to forget our other responsibilities. Playtime is good. Playing when we should be working is not good. Otters have plenty of fun slipping down their slides, but they know when to stop playing to hunt for food and take care of their families.

Jesus is always our example. He ate dinner with his friends. He attended a wedding. And He enjoyed little children. He showed us that our lives include playtime. Being playful pleases God, because it means we are enjoying the life He gave us. Good fun brings glory to Him.

Think

Why do you think God made animals that like to play?

Journal

Does the way you play honor God? List any ways you could change your playtime, if you need to.

Pray

Dear Lord, thank You for playtime. Please give me a merry heart and help me to do all things, even playtime, for Your glory. Amen.

For we are God's handiwork, created in Christ Jesus to do good works, which God prepared in advance for us to do.

Ephesians 2:10

An Otter Is
CREATIVE

Otters are so cute. They love to wrestle with each other and chase their own tails. They love to swim and dive, too. They fascinate me, and I watch them every time I get the chance. My family and I spend a lot of time at the otter exhibit when we visit the aquarium.

Not only are otters one of God's most adorable and playful creatures (they even sleep floating on their backs and holding hands with each other!), but they are also creative. They use tools, like the rocks they find in their surroundings, to pound open hard clams so they can eat. God made them to be creative, just like He made you to be creative.

We were formed in God's image. He is a creator, which is why we were made to be creative as well. God created the universe and everything in it out of nothing. At first there was darkness and then He made light. He also made big galaxies and tiny insects. He made all plants and oceans. He made every animal of the air, land, and water. His greatest and most prized creations, though, are you and me.

There is nothing in our world that didn't start as God's creation. We have it a little easier. We don't have to make

On land, river otters rely on their sense of smell. In water, they rely on their vision.

something from nothing. Like the otter, we can use our God-given surroundings in inventive ways. We can be resourceful in solving problems. We can use crayons, paint, or play dough to produce beautiful art. God gave us imaginations to be able to do those things.

He also wants us to use our creativity to help other people. Can you think of creative ways to help those around you? God created us along with good works, prepared in advance, for us to do. So whether you draw a picture for a grandparent to brighten his day, or you do your chores with a happy heart, you are doing the good works you were created to do.

You were made to be creative in all areas of your life. And just as you look at the otter and delight in his creativity, God looks at you and delights in how you use the creativity He gave you.

Think

How can you help a family member or friend by using the creativity God gave you?

Journal

Write about something that inspires you to be creative—a sunset, a song, the way a parent reads to you at bedtime. Describe what sparks creative ideas inside of you.

Pray

Dear God, I'm glad that You are a God of creativity. Thank You for making me creative in Your image. Help me to use my creativity to honor You. Amen.

a PANDA is

distinctive,

sensitive,

rare, and

a climber.

By this everyone will know that you are my disciples, if you love one another.

John 13:35

A Panda Is
DISTINCTIVE

There's no mistaking a panda! Sure, there are lots of different kinds of bears in the world, but only the giant panda has black patches on its eyes, black ears, black arms and legs, and white fur everywhere else. If you watch a panda at the zoo, you'll see that it constantly eats bamboo shoots and it sits in a slightly humped way, which makes it look like a giant teddy bear.

Everything about the panda makes it distinctive, meaning it's unique, different, and uncommon. There may be slight differences among panda bears, but every panda has these basic characteristics that set it apart from all other bears.

Did you know that God wants you to be as distinctive as a panda bear? It's true! God said that all His children should have distinctive characteristics, such as being known for our love for one another; being humble, gentle, and patient; living in peace with one another; loving God with all our heart, soul, and strength; and loving our neighbors as much as we love ourselves.

What do these characteristics have in common? They're all characteristics of God! That means God wants us to act like Him. That sounds difficult, doesn't it? The good news is that

Pandas have lived on Earth for two or three million years.

God's Spirit helps us to become more like Him the more we pray, read our Bibles, and worship.

Before knowing God, someone may act mean and selfish. But after beginning to follow God, that person will become kinder and will start to help others in need.

Before knowing God, someone may be sad and worried all the time. But after beginning to follow God, that person will be filled with joy and faith.

Being a follower of God doesn't make us perfect. We will still make mistakes. But we can try each day to display God's characteristics to everyone around us.

The panda bear is distinctive in every way, and you should be, too! Show others that you love God by displaying the qualities that come from following Jesus.

Think

The Bible says that Christians should be easily identified by how they love one another. How do you display love to your family and friends?

Journal

Write about a time when someone noticed your godly characteristics. Were you being kind, gentle, loving? How did it make you feel? How did the other person respond?

Pray

Dear Lord, thank You for calling me to be as distinctive as the panda bear. Help me to be more like You every day. Amen.

*A wicked person listens to deceitful lips;
a liar pays attention to a destructive tongue.*

Proverbs 17:4

A Panda Is
SENSITIVE

They don't really know kung fu, but curious, playful giant pandas do enjoy turning somersaults and solving bamboo puzzles to find hidden food. These bears look like 200-some pounds of black-and-white cuddliness. But if you spot a panda plodding along in your neighborhood, don't run up to it for a hug any more than you'd snuggle with a grizzly. They're still bears, with powerful jaws that bite hard and sharp claws that can tear through trees.

Here's something else not to do: yell. Pandas have sensitive ears. They communicate with each other more than any other bear, so they need to hear each other clearly. Pandas even detect ultrasonic sounds—pitches so high that the human ear can't hear them at all.

Zoologists believe one of the biggest dangers facing pandas in the wild is too much noise. When humans build too close to the damp, misty forests where pandas live, all the noise confuses a panda's sensitive ears. They stop getting together because they can't clearly hear each other talk.

God built your ears to be sensitive, too, but in a different way. The Bible warns us that too much noise—listening to

Pandas are a symbol of peace in China.

bad, wrong, hurtful, or gossipy things—threatens our hearts and souls. Bad things that you listen to pour ugly thoughts into your mind, which can plug the "ears" of your heart and prevent the good that God wants to do in your life.

In the Gospel, Jesus laments about people who won't let Him help them. He says they aren't really hearing with their ears or seeing with their eyes. He also says He wants to help and heal them. Jesus wants to help and heal us, too. We need open and ready ears to hear His voice so He can reach our hearts.

Let's be careful about to what and to whom we listen. We don't want the noise of bad things to drown out the gentle voice of God when He speaks to us.

Think

What kind of language, songs, and conversations are bad to listen to? How can you protect your sensitive ears from noise that hurts your soul?

Journal

Write about a time when you learned something good by finding a wise person and listening to what he or she had to say.

Pray

Dear Lord, thank you for giving me ears sensitive enough to hear You. Help me to be careful with what I hear so that I am always able to listen to You. Amen.

Are not five sparrows sold for two pennies? Yet not one of them is forgotten by God. ... Don't be afraid; you are worth more than many sparrows.

Luke 12:6-7

A Panda Is
RARE

Who doesn't love giant pandas? They are adorable, cuddly, beautiful black and white bears. Unfortunately, there are not very many pandas left in the world. There are currently only about 250 pandas in zoos. Most are found in China, where they are thought of as national treasures. Some experts believe there are as few as 1,000 giant pandas living in the wild.

Guess who else is rare? You! There is only one you! Even if you have an identical twin, your fingerprints are different. No one on this entire planet is exactly like you, and that means you're very rare.

When something is rare, it's also valuable. For example, China rents one of its rare pandas to zoos overseas for $2 million! That's a lot of money, and you're worth way more than a giant panda.

God knows every sparrow, every panda, and every person on Earth. Each one is a treasure to God, who created us all.

The Bible tells us that God gave His only Son to die upon a cross so that you could be saved and spend forever in heaven with Him. The cross proves your value! God sacrificed everything for you. How awesome is that?

Baby pandas are about the size of a stick of butter when they are born.

Like those adorable panda bears, you're rare, valuable, and treasured.

Think

Have you ever felt less than special or less than valuable? What caused you to feel that way?

Journal

Draw a picture of a cross. Write, "I'm rare. I'm valuable. I'm treasured," on the cross.

Pray

Dear God, thank You for treasuring me, and thank You for sending Your Son to die upon the cross so that I can spend forever with You in heaven. Amen.

No, in all these things we are more than conquerors through him who loved us.

Romans 8:37

A Panda Is

A CLIMBER

When you think of something soft and cuddly, I'll bet you think of a panda bear. But pandas are more than just the huggable creatures you see on television or in the zoo. Giant pandas can grow to over 100 pounds and be more than five feet long. Now that's what I call a big teddy bear!

One of the first things young pandas learn to do is climb. They begin climbing trees when they are just a few months old. By the time they are adults, pandas have been known to climb up to 13,000 feet to get their favorite food, bamboo leaves. (I'll bet you'd climb pretty far, too, for an ice cream cone or a cookie!)

How does a roly-poly panda bear have the ability to climb so high? God made pandas with fingernails that are soft at birth and grow thick and hard as they get older. Pandas use these long and strong fingernails to dig into the sides of trees. They do this to keep their fingernails from getting overgrown, but it also allows them to climb higher than any other bear. So even though pandas look chubby and slow, God has given them a just-right tool to make them awesome climbers.

Climbing trees takes work. Trying to decide the next branch to step on, using

Pandas' fur isn't soft. It's thick and wiry.

your muscles to pull you up, and overcoming your fear of being so high are just a few of the challenges.

Life sometimes brings hard things, like tree climbing, our way. Maybe someone teased you about your clothes at recess or about the sandwich you ate at lunch. You might be worried about the test you have tomorrow. Maybe you're wondering if you'll ever have a best friend. All of these are trees you have to climb.

Praying, reading God's word, talking to your parents or another trusted adult, and listening for God's voice are tools for when the climbing gets tough.

Like with the panda, it may not look like you are strong enough to climb the trees life puts in your way, but God has given you all you need to dig in and find the strength to do just that.

Think

Name one of your favorite Bible heroes who had some big trees to climb and what he or she did when faced with a challenge.

Journal

Which trees need climbing in your life right now? Make a list, and next to each one, write one thing you can do to find the right next step.

Pray

Dear Lord, thank You for giving me all I need to overcome the big trees in my life. Help me be a strong climber by learning Your word and listening to Your voice. Amen.

a SHEEP is

**hopeful,
obedient,
vulnerable, and
a listener.**

The next day John saw Jesus coming toward him and said, "Look, the Lamb of God, who takes away the sin of the world!"

John 1:29

A Sheep Is
HOPEFUL

With their thick wool and seemingly small bodies, sheep and their lambs polka-dot the green pastures of spring. When they are born, these frail creatures hardly have enough wool to cover their bodies, and must find their path to survival beneath the comfort of their mamas' love.

They appear to be meek and mild, but these animals are resilient. They withstand rain, snow, hail, and heat, as they persevere to the next day. They not only endure weather, but also predators, disease, and the challenge of finding food. These animals never lose hope. They keep going. Do you ever have days when it would be easy to give up and not have any hope?

God tells us that when we stand in the Lord, we rejoice in hope and all His glory. We do not fear or dread anything. The God of hope is with us and will not leave us or forsake us.

It's easy to not want to stand with God in faith and hope because of the elements we face. Maybe you've had really bad storms in your life, or predators have been pulling at you to give up. But you can place your hope in the Lord. He will renew your strength. You will soar on wings like eagles, run and not grow

When sheep are ill, they know which specific plants to eat to cure themselves.

weary, and walk and not be faint. Like the lamb beneath the sheep's thick wool, you will be comforted in God's hope and promise.

Whatever you're feeling today, remember the sheep in the pastures standing strong through spring showers pelting their wool coats and coyotes lurking in the shadows, waiting for a meal. Even with these threats, sheep do not waiver. They stand with strength. Sheep keep going.

Although they are confronted with many obstacles at birth, lambs are born with hope-filled hearts, even if they don't know it. They go straight for what they instinctively know is their means of survival, and that's their mamas, who have withstood the elements to be there for them.

As the lamb rests in the comfort of its mama's constancy, let us also rest in knowing the hope of the Lord will never leave us. Our Father set us free of our sins when He so loved the world that He sent His only begotten son, the Lamb of God.

Think

Recall a time when you felt like giving up. What pulled you down? What made you feel hopeful again?

Journal

What makes you feel hopeful?

Pray

Dear Lord, thank You for giving me hope in all circumstances. Help me believe in Your strength to carry me when I feel like giving up. Amen.

I am the good shepherd; I know my sheep and my sheep know me—just as the Father knows me and I know the Father—and I lay down my life for the sheep.

John 10:14-15

A Sheep Is
OBEDIENT

Sheep follow their shepherd. Like fluffy clouds puttering around the meadows, they flock behind their leader. To grassy fields, to streams of fresh water, sheep follow their shepherd to everything they need. They obey all that their shepherd directs them to do because they trust him.

God tells children to obey their parents. Just like a shepherd will guide his sheep to stay out of dangerous forests, your parents will tell you to hold their hands when you cross the street. Obeying them is important and good. It's what God calls you to do. As you follow their directions, it will also bring you joy.

Learning to obey your parents is a lot like learning to obey God. We all know that parents aren't perfect, though. Who is perfect? Jesus.

He is your best protector and your true shepherd. Jesus says that we, His sheep, can know Him just as closely as He knows God the Father.

A shepherd must know his sheep as individuals. He knows the personality of every little character on his field. Maybe Bob likes to chase butterflies. And

sheep can remember up to fifty sheep and human faces for up to two years.

Sally is the slowest grazer ever. A shepherd knows every quirk, in order to take care of his flock.

Knowing that they have such a caring leader, sheep are happy to obey their shepherd. They know that in his care, they don't need to be afraid. Whether you are obeying the leadership of your parents or following what Jesus wants you to do, obedience is something that makes God very happy.

If you're having a hard time obeying, ask God for help. Sometimes it feels difficult. Sometimes you might think that chasing a butterfly is more fun than following directions. But remember that your parents are guiding you to help you grow, and Jesus is shepherding you to be more like Him. As you trust in Him, He will help you to become an obedient sheep in His flock.

Think

> Who are the leaders in my life that God wants me to obey?

Journal

How can I show obedience to my parents this week?

Pray

Dear God, please help me to follow You and what You teach in the Bible. Please help me to obey my parents with a happy heart, like sheep following their shepherd. Amen.

*I am the good shepherd.
The good shepherd lays down his life for the sheep.*

John 10:11

A Sheep Is
VULNERABLE

Have you ever touched a big, woolly sheep? It's like they're covered in millions of thick cotton bolls! Farmers sell this wool to be made into warm materials, like clothes and blankets. Other farmers raise sheep for their milk, which is used to make special cheeses.

We get a lot of helpful products from sheep, which is why farmers have been raising them for thousands of years. However, there is one big problem with raising sheep: they're vulnerable to predators. That means the sheep can't defend themselves well from animals like bears and wolves. They don't have big horns or sharp teeth, and while they can run and kick, they're no match for stronger, faster animals. Sheep can even get really sick just from being frightened!

Fortunately, sheep have all the protection they need in the shepherd. It's the shepherd's job to guard the sheep day and night. Today, many shepherds use special alarms, guard dogs, and even guard llamas to help them protect their sheep from harm. But years ago, shepherds had only their staffs, long sticks with a curved end.

One of the most famous shepherds is David, who later became king of Israel. While watching over his flock, he had

Sheep wool differs in length and texture, depending on the climate where the sheep lives.

to fight off both a lion and a bear! David used a staff and a slingshot to kill the predators and save his flock. He was a very brave young man. When David told the story to King Saul, he credited God with delivering him from the beasts.

The most famous shepherd is Jesus. Although He never watched over actual sheep, He told His followers that He is the Good Shepherd. What does this mean?

Jesus knows that we are like sheep, vulnerable to bad things in this world, from bad habits to bad people. We just can't run away fast enough or fight hard enough on our own. But Jesus, our Shepherd, protects us. He keeps us safe and helps us get through difficult situations.

Your parents, teachers, and pastors also act like shepherds, protecting you to make sure you're safe. That's why it's so important to obey the trusted adults in your life.

The world is beautiful, but there are dangers out there. The good news is that there's no reason to be afraid, not with a Good Shepherd like ours!

Think

Sometimes when your parents tell you what to do, they're trying to keep you from getting hurt. Are you quick to obey them?

Journal

Write about a time when someone helped keep you safe.

Pray

Dear Lord, thank You for being the Good Shepherd! Please continue to watch over me and keep me safe through obedience to my parents, my shepherds here on Earth. Amen.

My sheep listen to my voice; I know them, and they follow me.

John 10:27

A Sheep Is
A LISTENER

Sheep and shepherds are mentioned 247 times in the Bible. Jesus is called the Good Shepherd, and as Christians, we are called His sheep. That's a really awesome example of our relationship with God, because sheep are really cool!

Sheep are very sensitive animals who are loyal to their shepherds. In fact, sheep are able to tell their shepherd's voice from all other voices. If two shepherds meet and their flocks mingle together, the sheep will have no problem knowing which shepherd to follow as soon as those two shepherds call.

It's the same way for us. As Christians, we know God's voice and hear Him over all of the other voices in our lives.

You might be thinking, I haven't ever heard God speak to me. But you probably have—just not in a big, loud voice. God speaks to us in different ways. Sometimes, you might be reading the Bible and a verse of Scripture will almost jump off the page. That's one way you know that God is trying to get a message to you. Other times, God will cause your pastor to say something that feels like it was

Sheep have four-chambered stomachs.

meant just for you. Still other times, God will use a friend, a family member, or even a song to speak to your heart.

Think of it like this: you have an "ear" in the middle of your heart. As a follower of Jesus, you hear His voice with your heart. The more you try to listen for His voice, the more you'll be able to hear Him. Like sheep, you'll become more sensitive to hearing His voice and to following the Good Shepherd.

Think

Do you set aside a special time each day to read the Bible? Remember, the more time you spend with God, the better you'll know His voice.

Journal

Write about a time when you heard God's voice. If you haven't ever heard God's voice, do you want to?

Pray

Dear God, please help me to hear Your voice over all of the other voices in my life. I want to know You more and to follow after You. Amen.

a **ZEBRA** is

**bold,
stubborn, and
an individual.**

So God created mankind in his own image, in the image of God he created them; male and female he created them.

Genesis 1:27

A Zebra Is
BOLD

Zebras are some of the boldest animals in Africa. They know what they're good at, and they do it well. Zebras like what they are, and they never try to be anything else. Zebras spend their lives on the grasslands and hills of Africa being the best zebras they can be.

While zebras may look like striped horses, there are some very big differences between the two animals. Zebras are found only in Africa, and they are wild. Unlike horses, zebras don't really like people, and you can't ride them. While they look cute and cuddly, zebras are not into being hugged. They also have a painful bite!

They are loyal to the other zebras in their herd, and they will come to help each other in times of trouble. Because zebras are so bold, they are also brave. Zebras have even been seen fighting off lions!

You can be just as bold as a zebra, because God designed and created you to be uniquely you. Just like the zebra is not supposed to be a horse, you are not supposed to be like anyone else. You are supposed to be you!

Sometimes you'll have a hard day. Sometimes you may not feel good enough or smart enough. Maybe a teacher

Zebras' stripes help them to camouflage themselves in the grass and to keep biting insects away.

asked you a question, and you didn't know the answer. Or maybe you couldn't find anyone to play with on the playground. That's okay. Everyone has hard days.

The next time you have a hard day, think about the zebra and how bold it is. And then remind yourself that you can be just as bold because of how God created you. You may not have black and white stripes, but God created you with even more amazing markings. You are unique and special. You can be bold because God made you exactly how He wanted you to be.

Think

What are some things you like about yourself? Why do you think God gave you those gifts?

Journal

Describe a time when you didn't feel very bold. Now describe a time when you did feel bold.

Pray

Dear God, thank You for making me just what You need me to be. Help me to be confident in Your design and grateful for my life. Amen.

Whoever is not with me is against me, and whoever does not gather with me scatters.

Matthew 12:30

A Zebra Is
STUBBORN

Zebras are unmistakable with their black and white stripes, long ears and face, and bray. Though we're very familiar with them, they are very difficult to domesticate. Zebras don't make the best pets. Not only are they wild animals, but they are also stubborn. Zebras are going to do what they want to do, in their way. When they lock their hooves in places, there's no budging them.

Maybe sometimes you are stubborn too. This means you just want to do it your way, and nothing else matters. Having these feelings is normal. But not being willing to budge can mean losing great opportunities or missing out on new things you might like even better than what you're used to.

God knows the plans He has for you, to prosper you and not harm you, to give you hope and a future. Sometimes it's hard to trust in God's plan. It can seem easier to lock our feet like a stubborn zebra and stick with what we know. But often in those situations, what's really driving us is fear, rather than love.

You can trust in the Lord. He asks you to work with Him, and not against Him. By letting go of being stubborn and ornery about change,

Zebras join other groups of animals, like wildebeests, to create larger herds for safety from predators.

you honor God. If you give a new way of doing something a chance, you might find it's an even better way. You never know what God has planned for you, but you can be sure it's going to be just what you need to draw closer to Him.

So instead of being a wildly undomesticated, stubborn zebra, stand strong and trust in the Lord. He wants the very best for you.

Think

What do you fear when you're being stubborn? How can you face those fears?

Journal

Write about a time when you just did not want to give in to doing something differently, but something made you try.

Pray

Dear Lord, thank You for knowing the plans You have for me. Please help me not to be stubborn and fearful of things I don't know, and to trust in You in all things. Amen.

Before I formed you in the womb I knew you, before you were born I set you apart; I appointed you as a prophet to the nations.

Jeremiah 1:5

A Zebra Is
AN INDIVIDUAL

Zebras are beautiful and unique creatures, known for their bold black stripes. Although there are three general stripe patterns among them, no two zebras have the exact same stripes. Just as no two snowflakes are exactly alike, no two zebras are exactly alike. It's the same with humans, too, of course. God created humans as complete individuals, with no two humans being exactly alike.

Just like each zebra has its own unique stripe pattern, you have your own unique look, personality, talents, and gifts. God created you with your exact height, your laugh, down to the last freckle and even the number of hairs on your head. He made you *you*, and He cares about the unique details that He gave you. You can be proud of how individual you are and know that you were created exactly the way He wants you to be.

You are one of a kind, just like the zebra. Some of us have dark skin, while others have light skin. Some have curly hair, while others have straight hair. Some need glasses, and some don't. Some wear braces, and some have straight teeth. Some people are tall, while others are short. Some speak up loudly, and others are soft-spoken. Some are great at sports, while others

Zebras sleep standing up.

excel in the arts. There is no one in the history of the world who is exactly like you and there never will be in the future.

Whenever you see a zebra, remember that the God in heaven who created both zebras and you loves what makes you an individual.

Celebrate your differences, because God created you on purpose and with a purpose. You are special and unique in His sight.

Think

What one-of-a-kind qualities can you think of in yourself, your closest friends, and your family members?

Journal

Write about your favorite animals and the differences that make them special. Describe what it would be like to have one as a pet in your home.

Pray

Dear God, thank You for giving me my unique gifts and a personality that only You could give. Amen.

Contributors

Michelle Medlock Adams is the author of the award-winning *C Is for Christmas*, as well as over ninety other books. Connect with her at her website, michellemedlockadams.com.

Janet L. Christensen is the author of the award-winning *Good Night, Fireflies* and *Cairo's Christmas Journey*. Visit Janet online at janetlchristensen.com.

Annette M. Clayton is a writer, reader, and blogger who loves books. Find out more at annettemclayton.com.

Amberly Kristen Clowe is the author of the Teeny Sweeney series, the first of which is *Teeny Sweeney and the Mustache Cash*. She'd love to connect with you at her website, amberlykristenclowe.com.

Burton W. Cole is the author of the Bash and Beamer series. You can visit him online at burtonwcole.com.

Amanda Flinn is a writer of children's books. Find her online at amandaflinn.com.

Neena Gaynor is a Kentucky beekeeper and writer. Learn more about her at wordslikehoney.com.

Jean Matthew Hall is the author of *God's Blessings of Fall*, the first in a series of picture books celebrating God's seasons. Connect with her at jeanmatthewhall.com.

Tori Higa is the author and illustrator of *The Christmas Color*. See more of her work at torihiga.com.

Janelle Higdon writes about beauty in Christ, and would be happy to connect at beautyinjesus.com.

Ashley L. Jones has always been curious about Jesus and His love. You can learn more about her at BigSisterKnows.com.

Rachel Pellegrino is the founder and publisher of Little Lamb Books. She hopes you'll share the lambie love at littlelambbooks.com

Jean Petersen is the author of the award-winning *Kind Soup*. Learn more about her at jeanpetersen.com.

Suzanne Reeves is a published writer, vibrant theater actress and director, and a proud native Texan. Follow her on Facebook @ThePerkyTexanWriter.

Patti Richards is an award-winning writer of books for children. Visit her online at pattigail1.com.

Shelly Roark is the award-winning author of *The Bubble Who Would Not POP!* and *Gracie Lou Wants a Zoo*. Connect with her at shellyroarkauthor.com.

Lindsay Schlegel is the editor-at-large for Little Lamb Books. Learn more about her at LindsaySchlegel.com

Debbie Spence is a writer who takes joy in the simple pleasures of life. Meet her on her website, debbiespence.com.

Works Cited

"30+ Amazing Animal Traits!" *Gentle World*, 27 Aug. 2015, gentleworld.org/30-amazing-animal-traits/.

"Amazing Animal & Insect Facts For Kids." *Cool Kid Facts*, 25 Sept. 2020, www.coolkidfacts.com/animals/.

"Animal Facts." *Animal Fact Guide*, 30 Dec. 2020, animalfactguide.com/animal-facts/.

Sciencing, sciencing.com/.

Traits Index

Aggressive	102	Gentle	30
Beautiful	80	Graceful	86
Bold	156	Hopeful	146
Brave	112	Humble	34
Clever	94	Independent	100
Climber	142	Individual	160
Courageous	110	Intelligent	118
Cranky	42	Joyful	62
Creative	132	Just	114
Curious	92	Kind	60
Dependable	18	Leader	108
Devoted	54	Lives in community	104
Diligent	12	Listener	152
Distinctive	136	Loving	56
Energetic	128	Mean	44
Faithful	52	Obedient	148
Flexible	122	Optimistic	50
Foresight	22	Pack-oriented	74
Friendly	126	Perceptive	120

Playful	130	Tough skin	46
Protective	98	Vulnerable	150
Protects the weak	76	Willing to Learn	64
Quick	90		
Quiet	32		
Rare	140		
Reliable	72		
Responsible	26		
Sacrificial	24		
Self-confident	82		
Sensitive	138		
Silly	36		
Sneaky	40		
Social	66		
Spunky	84		
Strong	70		
Strong for its size	14		
Stubborn	158		
Team player	16		

Scripture Verse Index

Genesis 1:27	A Zebra Is Bold	156
Deuteronomy 31:6	A Crocodile Has Tough Skin	46
Joshua 1:9	A Lion Is Courageous	110
Psalm 16:11	A Dolphin Is Joyful	62
Psalm 18:1	An Ant Is Strong for Its Size	14
Psalm 46:1	A Hippo Is Protective	98
Psalm 46:10	A Fox Is Quick	90
Psalm 133:1	A Hippo Lives in Community	104
Psalm 139:14	A Flamingo Is Self-Confident	82
Proverbs 1:8	A Bunny Is Silly	36
Proverbs 2:6	An Octopus Is Intelligent	118
Proverbs 3:24	A Lion Is Brave	112
Proverbs 6:6-8	An Ant Is Dependable	18
Proverbs 8:9	An Octopus Is Perceptive	120
Proverbs 16:3	A Dog Is Devoted	54
Proverbs 17:4	A Panda Is Sensitive	138
Proverbs 18:15	A Fox Is Curious	92
Proverbs 31:8	An Elephant Protects the Weak	76
Ecclesiastes 3:1	An Octopus Is Flexible	122
Isaiah 1:19	A Dolphin Is Willing to Learn	64

Jeremiah 1:5	A Zebra Is an Individual	160
Jeremiah 29:11	A Bee Has Foresight	22
Micah 6:8	A Lion Is Just	114
Zephaniah 3:17	A Flamingo Is Beautiful	80
Matthew 5:16	A Flamingo Is Spunky	84
Matthew 12:30	A Zebra Is Stubborn	158
Matthew 16:23	A Crocodile Is Sneaky	40
Luke 12:6-7	A Panda Is Rare	140
Luke 16:10	A Bee Is Responsible	26
John 1:29	A Sheep Is Hopeful	146
John 10:11	A Sheep Is Vulnerable	150
John 10:14-15	A Sheep Is Obedient	148
John 10:27	A Sheep Is a Listener	152
John 13:35	A Panda Is Distinctive	136
John 15:13	A Bee Is Sacrificial	24
Acts 4:33-34	A Flamingo Is Graceful	86
Romans 8:37	A Panda Is a Climber	142
Romans 15:13	A Dog Is Optimistic	50
1 Corinthians 1:9	An Elephant Is Reliable	72
1 Corinthians 10:31	An Otter Is Playful	130
1 Corinthians 12:12	An Ant Is a Team Player	16

1 Corinthians 12:26	An Elephant Is Pack-Oriented	74
2 Corinthians 5:7	A Dog Is Faithful	52
Galatians 5:22–23	A Hippo Is Aggressive	102
Ephesians 2:10	An Otter Is Creative	132
Ephesians 4:2	A Bunny Is Gentle	30
Philippians 4:4	A Crocodile Is Cranky	42
Philippians 4:13	An Elephant Is Strong	70
Ephesians 4:31	A Crocodile Is Mean	44
Colossians 3:12	A Dolphin Is Kind	60
Colossians 3:23–24	An Otter Is Energetic	128
1 Thessalonians 5:11	An Otter Is Friendly	126
1 Timothy 4:15	An Ant Is Diligent	12
Hebrews 13:1	A Dog Is Loving	56
James 1:5	A Fox Is Clever	94
James 3:13	A Bunny Is Humble	34
1 Peter 3:4	A Bunny Is Quiet	32
1 Peter 4:9	A Dolphin Is Social	66
1 John 4:16	A Hippo Is Independent	100
Revelation 5:5	A Lion Is a Leader	108

Lindsay Schlegel

Lindsay Schlegel, editor-at-large for Little Lamb Books, is a writer and editor with more than fifteen years' experience in publishing. She's worked in marketing, publicity, bookselling, and agenting, but her favorite role is editing, especially books as adorable as this one! Lindsay is also the author of *Don't Forget Say Thank You: And Other Parenting Lessons That Brought Me Closer to God* and the host of the podcast, *Quote Me*. She lives in New Jersey with her family, and can be found at LindsaySchlegel.com.

Katie Wekall

Katie Wekall is a children's book illustrator from South Carolina. She holds a degree in Elementary Education from UNC-Wilmington, and enjoys sharing her love of literature by teaching young minds. She also delights in using digital media to bring children's books to life and help instill a love of reading in kids. A passionate collector of art and all things Disney, Katie draws inspiration for her whimsical and colorful style from her students. Follow Katie on Instagram via @katie_illustrations.

Be the first to hear about NEW picture books and chapter books from Little Lamb Books!

Sign up for announcements about new and upcoming titles at:

https://littlelambbooks.com

@little_lamb_books   @littlelambbooks

@LittleLambBooks   @LittleLambBooks

@LittleLambBooks

Don't miss out on our family-friendly and faith-filled books for elementary, middle grade, and young adult readers!

little lamb
BOOKS
Shepherding the next generation of faithful readers

CPSIA information can be obtained
at www.ICGtesting.com
Printed in the USA
LVHW071112021121
702218LV00001B/13